# The Ultimate physique

# The Ultimate physique BODYBUILDING

with Bill Richardson *'Mr. World'*

by Bill Richardson and David Webster

Adam and Charles Black
London

Copyright © Bill Richardson and David Webster 1984

First edition 1984

Published by A & C Black (Publishers) Ltd,
35 Bedford Row, London WC1R 4JH, England

This book is copyright under the Berne Convention. All rights are reserved. Apart from any fair dealing for the purpose of private study, research, criticism or review, as permitted under the Copyright Act, 1956, no part of this publication may be reproduced, stored in a retrieval system, or transmitted in any form or by any means, electronic, electrical, chemical, mechanical, optical, photocopying, recording or otherwise, without the prior permission of the copyright owner. Enquiries should be addressed to the Publishers.

Design: Etchell & Ridyard

**Photograph credits**
The exercise photographs were taken especially for this book; the authors and publishers wish to thank John Kilburn of the Fitness and Fantasy Gymnasium, Bradford, for allowing his gymnasium to be disrupted for this purpose; also Jungeling Limited for the use of their equipment.

Other photographs are by Barry Dawson, Edward Hankey and Alex McKenna.

> Richardson, Bill
>  The ultimate physique.
>  1. Bodybuilding
>  I. Title   II. Webster, David, *1928–*
>  796.4'1   GV546.5
>
>  ISBN 0-7136-2448-5 (casebound)
>  ISBN 0-7136-2449-3 (paperback)

Typeset in 10/11pt Optima by PFB Art & Type Ltd, Leeds
Printed and bound in Great Britain at The Pitman Press, Bath

# Contents

1 **Bill Richardson — a profile** 7

2 **Bodybuilding — the state of the art** 14
   Organisations
   A note on the future

3 **General instruction** 29
   Apparel for training
   Ventilation
   Rest pauses
   Breathing
   Progression
   Specialisation
   Muscle work
   Curve of effort
   Foot spacing
   After exercising
   Relaxation

4 **Bodybuilding exercises** 36
   Arms
   Shoulders
   Chest
   Abdominals
   Back
   Legs
   Thighs
   Calves

5 **Workout routines** 82
   Beginners' schedule
   Intermediate schedule
   Semi-advanced schedules
   Advanced routines

6 **Nutrition for bodybuilders** 86
   Protein requirements
   Supplements
   A personal diet

7 **Drugs** 88

8 **Contest preparation — peaks and troughs** 97
   Pitfalls on the way to the peaks

9 **Posing** 101
   The basics of good posing
   Planning your poses
   Displaying the body parts
   Music
   Photographic physique studies

10 **Positive thinking** 117
   The goal of improvement
   Just a little bit more

11 **Psychology of competition** 121
   Being psyched-out
   Psyching up
   How not to be psyched-out

12 **A final word** 125

   **Glossary of basic terms** 126

   **Index** 128

# The Ultimate Physique

# 1 Bill Richardson — a profile

The little island of Aruba, 15 miles off the Venezuelan coast and to the west of Curaçao, is famed for its sunshine, rock formations and monolithic boulders. Born in this little known paradise was Bill Richardson, a man who typifies his birthplace, being of a sunny, happy disposition but rock-hard in resolve and in physique. It is perhaps paradoxical that an unknown from a tiny speck on the globe should gain the titles of both Mr World and Mr Universe, becoming one of the most perfectly built men of all time, but this amazing character — who long ago became a British citizen — is himself a paradox.

His family left Aruba when he was three years old to go to St Kitts, and there the Richardsons lived for a further six years. When he was nine, Bill and his family came to Britain, which for them in 1956 was a land full of promise and hope. Settling in Yorkshire, Bill enjoyed his English schooling although, truth to tell, academic aspects received far less attention from him than sports, in which he excelled. He became very competent in swimming, football, cricket and, most of all, gymnastics. At every possible opportunity Bill persuaded his class teachers to let him do extra sports practice: 'Please Miss, I must go to football training'; 'Miss, I am wanted in the gym this morning.' The teachers were understanding, and encouraged him to work hard in these physical activities; after school he had little difficulty in getting work as a swimming instructor, and then as a masseur.

In 1970 he made the most important decision of his life: he decided to take up weight-training.

In Leeds the path to the pinnacles of bodybuilding had been trodden by Reg Park, who had taken the titles of Mr Britain and Mr Universe before departing for sunnier climes — a reversal of the pattern followed by Bill. There is an obscure link between these two enthusiasts, because the Gateway to Health gym, with which Reg was associated, turned out to be Bill's first proper training venue.

Like Reg, he was always interested in strength as well as in muscle-size, and the heavy weights he used soon made young Richardson one of the strongest men in the north of England. He was invited to enter an arm-wrestling contest on TV if he would compete using his left hand. He accepted and won easily, and this put him in line for the major open contest the following year, this time with the right hand: again he won without too much bother. 'Greats' such as Tony Fitton and Andy Deva were among those defeated in these events.

In 1970 he entered his first physique contest, the novice Mr Yorkshire event, and although his physique was by then well above average he did not have any knowledge of competition procedure or posing.

'The night before the competition everybody in the gym was trying to help by telling me what to do,' Bill recalls. 'I got a lot of conflicting advice — which was most confusing. It gave me the surprise of my life when I won. Strangely enough, most of the comments were not about my muscularity or definition but about the size of my neck and this, along with my forearms, is an area I never need to exercise specifically.'

*Reg Park in one of his classic poses*

The following year he faced stiffer opposition, coming fourth in the Mr North-East England contest, but he moved up a place each year until in 1973 he won the title as well as the Mr Yorkshire award.

It took a further five years' hard training and competition experience before he won the Mr United Kingdom title and the even more coveted Mr Britain competition, the physique event with the longest pedigree in the world. In 1978, after this British Championship, he was selected

# The Ultimate Physique

for the European finals, winning the amateur Mr Europe. Things were really hotting up for Bill: he was making his presence felt in the main contests, his pictures were regularly featured in national and international magazines, and he had a growing army of fans. During a sojourn in the most physique-conscious area in the world he became Mr California 1980, emulating the all-time 'greats' who had won this title as a step towards the premier Mr Universe award.

History did indeed repeat itself some six weeks later: Mr California became the new amateur Mr Universe. A further six weeks later, having left the 'Simon Pure' ranks of the amateurs, he won the professional European Championships for the first time, a feat he has repeated since then.

Prizes and honours galore came his way. Apparently only one ambition remained for the now internationally renowned physique champion, the professional Mr World title, but between him and this goal stood the unbeaten and supposedly unbeatable Kawak, a phenomenal French-Algerian. At the great contest held in Saarbrucken, West Germany, before a capacity audience, the Gods of Olympus smiled on the black Adonis of Britain. History records that he once more did what has become second nature to him — he reached the target he had set himself.

Bill Richardson was Mr World.

# BILL RICHARDSON — A PROFILE

*Ian Lawrence (Scotland)*

## Gentle giant with a heart of gold

Bill Richardson's 'track record' speaks for itself. He is the most successful and popular British bodybuilder of the past decade, and many would extend this to say that he is the greatest of all time. With such a string of amateur and professional titles behind him, including the coveted Mr Universe and Mr World awards, it is easy to see why he has so many ardent fans. The 'Black Hulk', as he is nicknamed by his admirers, is idolised wherever he goes, and his charisma is due not entirely to his out-of-this-world physique but also to his overall impact — the whole man is impressive, totally unspoiled by success and attractive to both sexes.

While inevitably his lifestyle is dominated by things physical, it is interesting, before reading of his training methods, to study Bill Richardson's character, philosophies and behaviour away from the posing rostrum and the spotlights.

In the working situation, we find Bill in an occupation for which he is admirably suited: for many years he has been the Chief Security Officer in the Arndale Shopping Centre, Bradford. Today his patch is a pretty quiet one, the disruptive elements preferring to give him a wide berth. Before big Bill took on the job, the centre was a real trouble spot, with gangs of youths creating havoc, but soon all that changed. It is my guess that Bill achieved this by the power of his personality and by generating respect, rather than by the application of his physical power.

He takes the occasional knife-carrying individual in his stride, without any hassle. 'It's all in a day's work, and there's no use getting excited about it. I prefer to use my nervous and physical energy in more positive ways,' says Bill. The newspapers describe his role much more dramatically, with, for example, the *Daily Mirror* headlining: MR UNIVERSE CRUSHES A CRIME WAVE.

At the time of going to press, Bill is in the process of moving to Holland to take up new and interesting work there.

Radio and TV stations frequently seek Bill's participation in their programmes, and he enjoys communicating in this way. He needs only a brief question or lead, and he will give a relevant, articulate reply with considerable authority. This is in marked contrast to the muscle-head image given to bodybuilders by some media men.

Since he is so much in the public eye, it is natural that such an affable character is in great demand to be a guest 'personality' at shows, for fund-raising and for a whole host of charitable functions. This Mr Universe takes his title very seriously, and he feels it is his duty to co-operate wherever he can. As a result, his efforts have helped tremendously on a great many occasions. For example, he pulled a double-decker bus around a supermarket car park for a playground group that was raising money for the Royal National Lifeboat Institution. Bill has judged all kinds of competitions, presenting prizes at sporting contests of all kinds, even sponsored pram races for hospitals.

One heart-warming incident illustrates the high regard in which he is held by his peers. Bill was asked to go to Scotland to present an award to Ian Lawrence, that country's greatest competitor and one of Bill's rivals — in the best possible sense, for although they meet on-stage with intense rivalry, there is mutual respect and friendship too. Bill willingly agreed to appear at the presentation in Ian's honour and went up on stage well prepared to sing the praises of the young Scot. To his utter astonishment the tables were neatly turned: in reality it was a well planned surprise to show Scotland's appreciation of Bill Richardson's contribution to bodybuilding. A packed hall cheered him to the echo, and he received plaudits from the most notable authorities in the sport.

David Mitchell, the official responsible for the event, said: 'Bill nearly fell through the floor. He had absolutely no idea he was to be honoured in this way and he had willingly travelled hundreds of miles to support Ian Lawrence. Bill is one of the nicest bodybuilders I have ever met and certainly the strongest.'

David went on to recall how on arrival in Milan for a competition he had been very amused when Bill, walking ahead of him, had immediately attracted the attention of the Italians. As it was a cold winter's day, Bill was wearing a furry jacket and looked about four feet wide. One chap's eyes seemed to bulge right out as he stood rooted to the spot. 'Mama Mia! Mama Mia!' he was muttering to himself as David Mitchell passed. Bill often has that sort of effect on people.

Oscar Heidenstam, secretary of the National Amateur Bodybuilders Association, is another supporter who has been acquainted with Bill for many years. When discussing the appeal of this champion Oscar said: 'It's easy to understand Bill's popularity as, apart from his muscles, he has many other qualities. He is brave, kind and has a great sense of humour.

'When in London for a contest, Bill was returning to his hotel late at night when he spotted an attempt to mug a petrol-station attendant. He immediately intervened and scattered the muggers, who did not enjoy the treatment he meted out to them.

'Not all his escapades finish on such a triumphant note. Once, when he chased and caught a woman who had been shoplifting on a rather grand scale, she fought and struggled like a wildcat. So, using the minimum of force, he put her over his shoulder and carried her back to the store. Outraged, she leaned down and bit him hard on his behind. Bill was more hurt than angry, and terribly embarrassed about showing the court proof of the assault!

'Bill has given us lots of laughs on various trips. When we landed in France on one occasion the first people we met were two black chaps. "It's just like being back in Bradford," cracked Bill, in his broad Yorkshire accent and with an equally broad grin.

'Yes, we all like Bill Richardson very much, and you can quote me on this.'

Coming from Heidenstam, a man who has met all the world's top physique stars, this is indeed a great compliment.

In bodybuilding circles it is widely known that Bill Richardson is one of those bodybuilders whose muscles function as well as they look. The huge weights he handles give ample proof of his strength, and the length and number of workouts, seven days a week, testify to his muscular endurance. On top of his weight-lifting routines, Bill clocked up nearly 100,000 miles on his bicycle in ten years, and was an undefeated champion in arm-wrestling. The 'Black Hulk' is one of the elite superhumans listed in the *Guinness Book of Records* since in 1979 he broke the world record in barrow-pushing, having pushed a load of 289 bricks weighing over a ton, 2,347 lb (1064.5kg) to be precise. This he pushed the stipulated 20ft using a very ordinary looking barrow, although it must have been an exceptionally strong one to carry 1.05 tons.

Although he does not have a 'circus strong-man' act, Bill often includes a few entertaining strength feats in his guest appearances. He does this in his own particular style, very much underplaying his abilities — a fact that only becomes clear when the audience begins to participate in the fun.

Bill invites some of the biggest and most powerful spectators to test the weights, and proceeds to show them how it is done. Without ever putting the hand

## BILL RICHARDSON — A PROFILE

*Bill's record-breaking feat of pushing a wheelbarrow carrying over a ton of bricks*

microphone down, he gives a running commentary throughout the lifts, the first of which is with a big old-fashioned globe dumb-bell. Here he lifts the awkward object with one hand, pressing it several times as he gives some hints on how to make it easier, then replaces it on the floor as gently as if it were a basket of eggs. It seems so simple that he has little difficulty in enticing weightlifters from the audience to display their strength and skill.

To the astonishment of all, *nobody* can duplicate Bill's lifts, and some can't even lift the dumb-bell from the floor. This is not as strange as it may seem, because this particular weight has an interesting history as a challenge to champions. It is one of three made in the 'Golden Age of Strength' for Tom Inch, a professional performer officially recognised as Britain's Strongest Man. A mistake was made by the manufacturer, who thought that such heavy weights would require thick handles, and this of course made them unliftable by any except supermen. An essential requirement to have any chance of bringing these weights to the shoulder is phenomenal grip and forearm strength. Bill has these attributes, so he has no problem with his dumb-bell from the original set of three, which passed from Tom Inch to Reg Park, former Mr Universe and hero of Hercules films.

Our modern Hercules has a great sense of humour, and another of his stunts demonstrates

The Ultimate Physique

# BILL RICHARDSON — A PROFILE

his love of a laugh. Bill has a beer barrel which he lifts overhead in various ways, yet when others try to copy him the barrel appears to develop a life and will of its own and revolves out of their grip, or spins uncontrollably, refusing to go overhead as it did for the champion bodybuilder. The secret, if it can be described as such, is that the barrel is partly filled with water, which moves in a completely unpredictable fashion inside the barrel. It takes all-round strength, without any weak links, to master and control this kind of unstable weight. The unrehearsed antics and comic facial expressions of those who attempt to lift the barrel are a source of mirth and light relief in a 'heavy' show. Bill has a happy knack of getting everybody to laugh together rather than some being laughed at, and he always finishes by ensuring that the audience express their appreciation of those who have been plucky enough to try their strength.

This Yorkshire man of iron makes no pretence to be an intellectual, yet he constantly receives letters from enthusiasts asking for advice and from organisers wanting him to appear in seminars, not only in this country but in others as well.

His sagacity in matters of training is well recognised, and this book is the result of numerous requests from those who cannot contact Bill personally. It contains the wisdom distilled during tens of thousands of training hours by a human dynamo who is right at the top of his field.

DPW

## 2 Bodybuilding — the state of the art

A beautiful physique is universally admired. Few would dispute this, but what varies considerably is personal taste as to what constitutes a beautiful physique. The concepts of physical beauty as portrayed in the statues of ancient Greece have remained with us over the centuries, and there are enough variations, from massive Hercules to shapely Apollo, to suit all individual preferences.

The creativity of the Greek sculptors using stone, hammer and chisel has now been substituted by that of the modern bodybuilder using his own body, weights and cables: each is a craftsman in the true sense. The physique artist, who uses live, human flesh, begins with nature's masterpiece as his raw material.

The modern bodybuilder's craft is now extremely refined, and to be successful the body which he creates must have a widely accepted blend of the four Ss: *s*ymmetry, *s*hape, *s*ize and *s*eparation. Let us examine what physique connoisseurs and competition judges mean by these terms.

A *symmetrical* physique is one which is evenly balanced. The large upper body and relatively underdeveloped legs of a trapeze artist would not rate as highly as a more moderately developed person whose limbs were in proportion to the torso. Many otherwise good physiques have been spoiled by a weakness in one area upsetting the whole balance of the physique.

Symmetry is often confused with *shape*, but there are clear distinctions. Shape concerns the flowing contours of the body — for example, broad shoulders and a deep chest narrowing to a muscular waist, or thick arms and forearms tapering to trim joints.

*Size* is self explanatory, but the knowledgeable person looks not only for fully rounded contours in the belly of the muscle but at the way these muscles 'tie-in' or blend with the surrounding muscle groups; for example, how the upper pectorals of the chest co-ordinate with the deltoids, and how these shoulder muscles tie-in with the arms. There must be not only size but density: the derogatory term 'cream puff muscles' implies a lack of muscular density and ability, qualities which bodybuilders strongly desire.

Muscular bulk on its own rates badly in modern bodybuilding: there must be *separation* of the muscles, and this takes two forms. Historically, 'muscular definition' was the quality of showing each individual muscle clearly outlined, but in recent years standards have changed considerably and now, not only must the muscle be seen clearly, the various *parts* of the muscle must have separation, so that the striations and cross-striations are clearly visible. Coupled with this is the very modern demand for 'vascularity', the showing of veins, which would most certainly have been frowned upon by the Greeks.

I have grown to admire practitioners of the modern art of bodybuilding because, as well as being artists, they have a knowledge of anatomy, physiology, nutrition, kinetics and bio-mechanics. They are artists, craftsmen and scientists with the dedication and motivation of international athletes. Knowledge in itself is useless: in this activity there has to be really hard physical work for many hours a day, month after month and year after year, to become a champion. Little wonder that relatively few become superstars in this sphere.

In addition to artistic considerations, there are competitive and commercial aspects which ignite controversy in gyms throughout the world. Many would have us believe that bodybuilding can gain international credibility only via the image of a competitive sport which has recognition from games and sports organisations. This may or may not be the case: my view is that bodybuilding is partly art and partly sport. However, it matters not whether I and those like me try to transcend Michelangelo by working on the more difficult medium of flesh rather than on stone or, alternatively, strive to become sporting heroes. In terms of competition, whereas in some sports there are no real winners, only survivors, in bodybuilding *every* contestant is a winner, with prizes of good health, fitness, vitality and self-confidence — priceless assets in a century of struggle and stress.

There are great similarities between bodybuilding and both sport and art: as in sport there is a

BODYBUILDING — THE STATE OF THE ART

The Ultimate Physique

bodybuilders but by the muscle-moguls who sell magazines, equipment and food supplements or who push drugs. This is one of the hardest pills we must swallow!

*Tom Inch, an early world middleweight champion weightlifter. Until the 1940s bodybuilders and weightlifters took part in the same physique contests. As mentioned on page 11, Bill has inherited one of Tom Inch's 'superman' dumb-bells*

need for dedicated training towards national and world titles; as with art success depends, in the final analysis, largely upon personal preferences, with different connoisseurs making slightly different choices.

In both spheres, for every person who makes a fortune there are many thousands practising the activity who get no financial returns whatsoever. The greatest gains, in monetary terms, are made not by practising

## Organisations

One of the most disturbing things about bodybuilding today is the proliferation of organisations claiming to be *the* governing body of the sport.

The National Amateur Bodybuilders Association (abbreviated to NABBA) is the organisation I support. It has been in this field for well over thirty years and, through Britain's *Health and Strength* magazine, has had links with major British physique contests since as long ago as 1930 and with the Mr Universe contest since it was first held in 1948.

In America, the Amateur Athletic Union organised the major physique contests, including the Mr America event, but the bodybuilders became disenchanted when they found themselves being treated as second-class citizens in comparison with the weightlifters, whose events they shared. Because of this, the International Federation of Bodybuilders gained in strength and there were many bitter battles between the two organisations and their related magazines, belonging to the York-based Bob Hoffman on the one hand and to the Weider Brothers on the other.

To confuse the issue still further, the Americans also had the World Bodybuilding Guild, which for some fifteen years in the 1960s and 1970s had Mr World contests. The struggles and squabbles between the various organisations have gone far beyond rivalry, on several occasions ending up in court.

In recent years yet another element has been introduced into American bodybuilding. 'Natural' bodybuilding associations have sprung up for those who do not take drugs and who do not wish to compete with people who use such artificial substances.

Meantime, in Europe, the Fédération Internationale Haltérophile et Culturiste, an organisation looking after world weightlifting and bodybuilding, decided to concentrate on lifting and ceased holding physique contests. Not unnaturally, the French and their continental neighbours wanted a continuing interest at top international level, and so the World Amateur Bodybuilding Association was formed. This organisation was loosely linked with NABBA, whose international competitions had continued to attract the very best physiques in the world. The great John Grimek was the first of a marvellous line of champions; other NABBA champions include Steve Reeves, Reg Park, Jack Delinger and Mickey Hargitay, husband of the ill-fated Jayne Mansfield. Every national champion seeking international recognition entered — and still enters — the Mr Universe contest, and it is worth remembering that it was the prestige of this series that first attracted Arnold Schwarzennegger of Austria, Franco Columbu of Italy, and America's Frank Zane, Bill Pearl, Chris Dickerson, Boyer Coe and

# The Ultimate Physique

*Above: Bill, having been voted NABBA Mr Universe 1980*

Dennis Tinerino. All these topliners and many more were NABBA champions, and I am proud to be in the company of such illustrious predecessors.

I do not think the various associations will ever get together, but I have made my choice and can compete at all levels without hindrance.

Just to complete the picture, there are now women bodybuilders whose aims roughly parallel those of the men. Although there have long been muscular ladies and figure contests, it is only in the recent past that we have had competitions for women with criteria closely resembling those for male bodybuilders.

Couples competitions, with male and female partners posing together, round off the range of events open to the fraternity. My wife has taken part with me in competitions, and working up a pairs-posing routine has been a real challenge as well as, eventually, a rewarding experience — although not without its trials and tribulations. It has introduced an element of teamwork into what I always thought was a purely personal, individual activity. This has been a bonus to me, giving the art a new and added interest.

## A note on the future

This, then, is my perspective of bodybuilders and bodybuilding at the present time, but I would like to make an observation and a speculation. The modern bodybuilder has created an interest in the male physique which has been unknown since the days of the classical Greek statues. The female body, on the other hand, has become identified with erotic fancies and sexual desire. I like to think that women bodybuilders and couples competitions could bring an improving influence to bear on this situation. Male paintings and statues are usually of an athletic, virile or healthy nature whereas the female body is more often exploited in sexually titillating situations, ranging from 'page 3' glamour in some newspapers to blatant pornography. Perhaps the swing of the pendulum towards the ultimate in female development will result in a healthier appreciation of the female body in its own right rather than as a sex object.

That would be a rare achievement for bodybuilding.

# 3 General instruction

Since boyhood, the words 'health', 'strength', 'muscles' and 'fitness' have been inextricably linked in my mind, and so I have a mental picture of exercises and bodybuilding resulting in a healthy life. Unfortunately, this is not necessarily so: only if the subject is taught properly will there be this great benefit. As in other parts of our lives, there are always some who will have tunnel vision: there are bodybuilders who see the subject in a very narrow way and ignore the finer points and basic factors which give the muscles *quality* as well as *quantity*.

When writing this book, it was very tempting to go straight into exercises and advanced principles instead of starting with the more elementary aspects, but after some reflection I decided that even the more advanced enthusiasts benefit by occasionally getting back to basics. So, at the risk of 'teaching granny to suck eggs', I review here some of the primary training principles.

## Apparel for training

Freedom of movement is a prime requirement for workouts, and all superfluous clothing should be discarded. You need to have with you a change of clothing, for if you train properly you will perspire, and you should not leave the gym with sweat-dampened togs — which will soon begin to attract attention in the least pleasant way. Clothing made from natural fibres such as cotton is very much better than nylon or terylene. Clothing sometimes aids concentration: you may get better results in terms of full contraction if you watch the muscles at work and so, if there are no draughts and if the gym is warm enough, you can discard your tracksuit or sweatshirt for this purpose.

The hygienic side should not be forgotten. It is best to wear a garment or to place your towel on the bench before doing any bench exercises. Acne and such skin complaints are not unknown in fitness and health circles and, when you consider that your pores are open during training, the need for hygienic practice becomes self-evident.

## Ventilation

The British climate, being cold, tends to make us keep all windows and doors shut. It is certainly necessary to avoid draughts when training, but there should nevertheless be good ventilation to get rid of the large quantities of carbon dioxide and body odours which fill the air when a group of people are training very hard. Good fresh air will help you to recuperate between sets and give you energy if you walk around breathing fully.

It goes without saying that there should be no smoking in the gym — indeed, there is absolutely no doubt whatsoever that smoking is detrimental to health. Most of those who contract lung cancer, heart disease, cancer of the bladder and other such deadly complaints are smokers. Cigarettes have no place in bodybuilding.

## Rest Pauses

The group or set system is the basis of all weight-training. It is important to note that the effect of 60 repetitions is very different when it is made up of 4 sets of 15 reps. from its effect if done as 1 set of 60 reps.; the latter is much more conducive to muscular endurance than to muscle building. Most bodybuilders work in repetitions varying from 6 to 15 or 20 and with 3 groups to 10 groups, depending on the specific requirements, the part of the body being worked, and the phase of training.

These matters will be discussed in greater depth in other parts of this book, but at this stage it is necessary to consider just how much time there should be between sets. For a start, avoid like the plague any of those characters who get involved in discussions and conversations between sets, or even between exercises. Leave all this until the workout is over. Between sets and exercises you should concentrate on recovering and preparing for the next set. Changing weights or standing by for and encouraging training partners are acceptable activities, but as soon as breathing has dropped back to a comfortable level you should get on with the next set.

The fitter you are the faster you will recover.

## Breathing

It may seem a nonsense to discuss such a natural process as breathing, but it is a fact that

correct breathing during exercise is extremely important, and a great many people do not breathe correctly — with results which we shall mention later. Generally, but not always, you should inhale as the effort is made and exhale as the weight is lowered under control.

The action of lifting the chest should be matched with an inhalation, and sometimes you may utilise this as a physique-building aid. When lowering dumb-bells slowly — for example, in bent-arm laterals or flying exercises — significant effort is required. A deep inhalation will raise your chest with an action which will help stretch the costal cartilage between your ribs and sternum (breast bone), thus deepening the chest cage. Some bodybuilders at this stage recommend a quick inhalation and another breath as you raise the weights.

You must always avoid holding your breath for any great length of time. In maximum efforts it is sometimes necessary to work on a solid base, and here you should take a breath quickly before lifting and let it out quickly at the end or after the exercise. It is at such times that there is the greatest danger of dizziness or blacking-out. The latter is known as the 'Valsalva effect', and is most common when there has been hyperventilation (continuous very deep inhalations) followed by the blood flow to brain and heart being impaired. Careful breathing, as outlined, without holding the breath will help avoid such distress.

## Progression

Constantly try to improve by using either more weight, more repetitions or even by adding another set or another exercise to your workout. There comes a time for the more mature bodybuilder when this is no longer possible; however, by now they will possess superlative physiques and have achieved their full potential.

For the vast majority of people some sort of progression is usually possible. This can be done very gradually, as the following examples indicate, starting with an exercise using 3 sets of 10 repetitions each with 100 lb (45.4kg).

| Simple Progression | $10 \times 100, 10 \times 100, 10 \times 100 = 3,000$ lb (1,361kg) |
| --- | --- |
| | $10 \times 100, 11 \times 100, 10 \times 100 = 3,100$ lb (1,406kg) |
| | $11 \times 100, 11 \times 100, 10 \times 100 = 3,200$ lb (1,451kg) |
| | $11 \times 100, 11 \times 100, 11 \times 100 = 3,300$ lb (1,497kg) |

Using the same sort of single-rep. progression, you can reach 15 reps. for 3 sets, totalling 4,500 lb (2,041kg). By adding a fourth set of, initially, just 10 reps. you would total 5,500 lb (2,495kg). When you reach 4 sets of 15 you get 6,000 lb (2,722kg) — twice as much work as at the start.

The next progression could be by adding 5 lb (2.27kg) for your first three sets:

$15 \times 105, 15 \times 105, 15 \times 105,$
$15 \times 100 = 6,225$ lb (2,824kg).

So it goes on in easy stages, adding one rep., one set or 5 lb (2.27kg). An added exercise gives the biggest increase in work, next a further set, then a rep., and finally the added weight, but it is the last of these which adds quality to the workout.

## Specialisation

If you are determined to reach the highest levels as a physique contestant you must concentrate on the activity to the exclusion of regular participation in any other demanding exercise. It is right and proper to do some cycling, jogging, swimming, etc., if you enjoy such activities but they should be complementary to your

# The Ultimate Physique

workouts and not *instead* of them; they should be kept at a level which will still allow you to have ample energy for lifting.

Even within bodybuilding, people often specialise further, concentrating on qualities such as definition or on a particular muscle group. Specialisation is sometimes necessary to bring under-par areas up to scratch or to add a highlight to the physique, and in such cases is to be commended. However, there are also pitfalls in specialisation. Avoid featuring your favourite exercises to the exclusion of others — it's so easy to become a one-exercise fanatic, with the bench press and curl being the hot favourites as the most overused exercises. Men with good arms greatly enjoy doing curls, and keep on curling as their arms get bigger and bigger and the rest of their body is overshadowed. Variety of work, keeping good balance in the development of all body parts, is the way to success and to all-round health and strength.

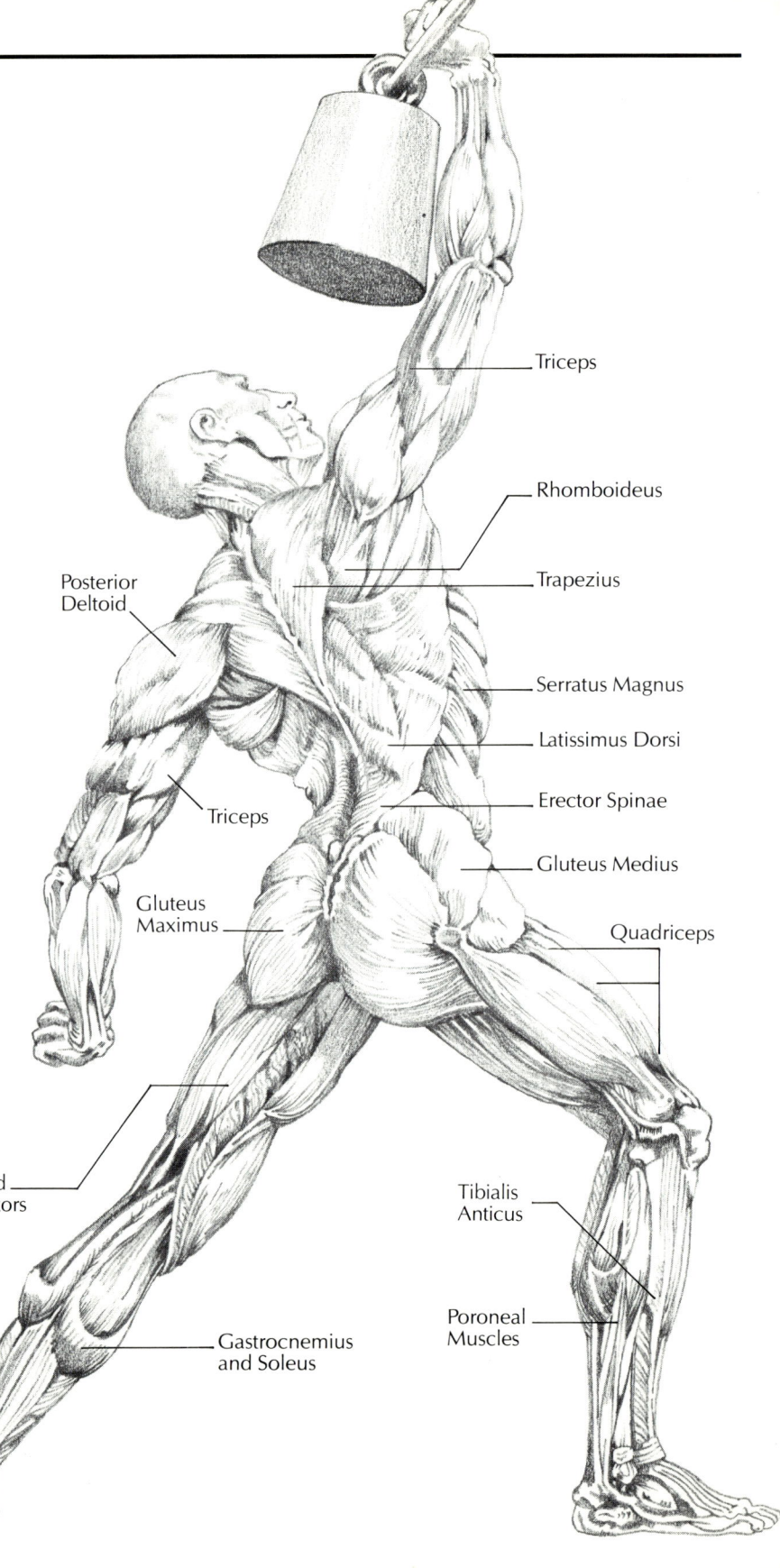

GENERAL INSTRUCTION

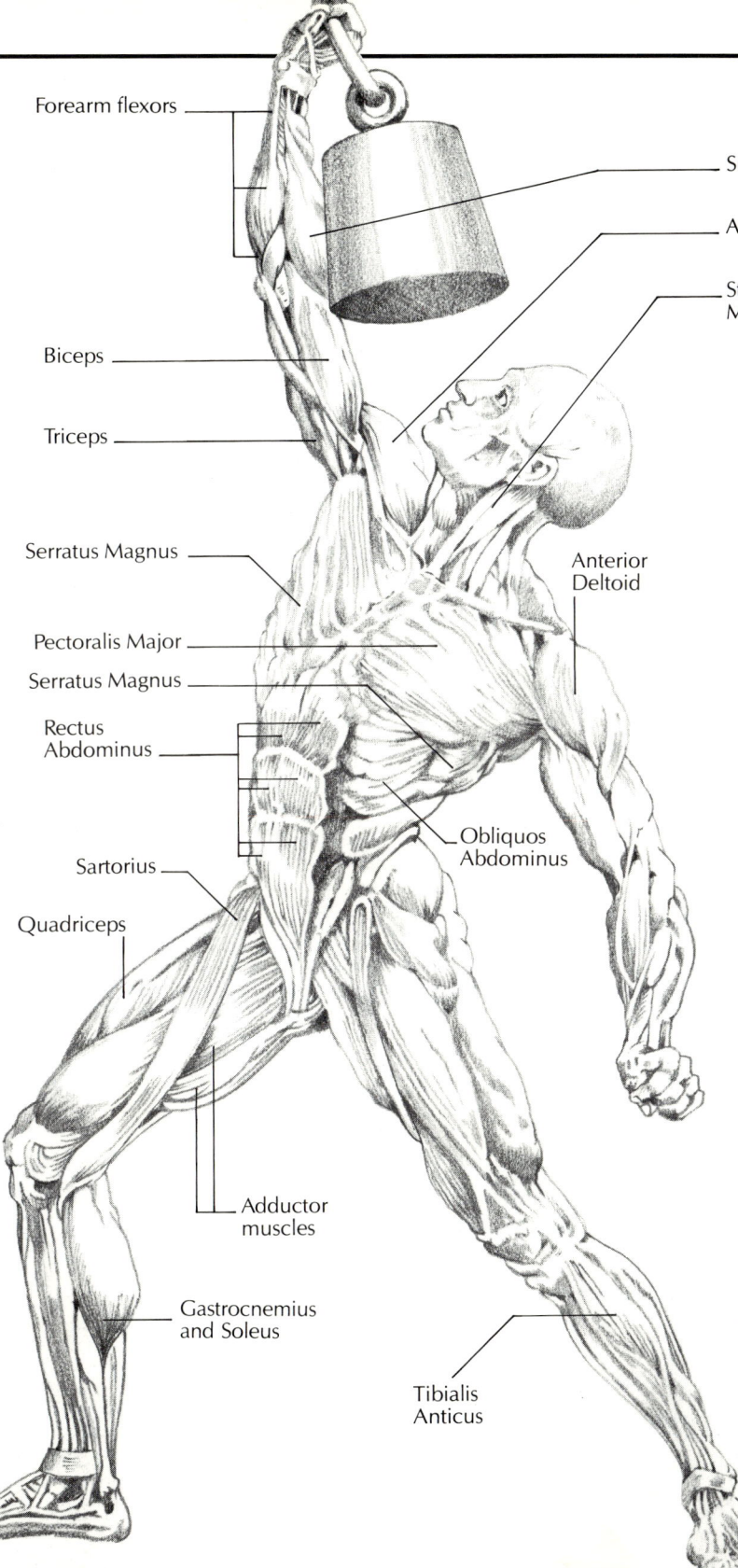

**Muscle work**

The last thing I want to do is to become too technical for readers, and so throughout this book jargon and technicalities are kept to the absolute minimum. However, in order to get across one particularly important principle I must explain an aspect of muscle-building which requires the use of a few less common words and which demands just a little thought.

Our muscles can work in different ways when we lift weights, when we hold weights in required positions and when we lower them *under control*.

When we lift a barbell or dumb-bell in an exercise, the working muscles actively shorten against the resistance of the weight. See how the biceps bunch up as you curl the bar, and note how the pectorals shorten and thicken as the weight is raised when you are doing the bench press. The same thing happens in all similar exercises. This active shortening against resistance is called *concentric* work.

Quite different muscle work is involved in lowering a weight slowly and *under control*. In this case there is *eccentric* muscle work, which simply means that the working muscle is actively *lengthening* against the resistance. This is a very important point, because a lot of bodybuilders

33

# The Ultimate Physique

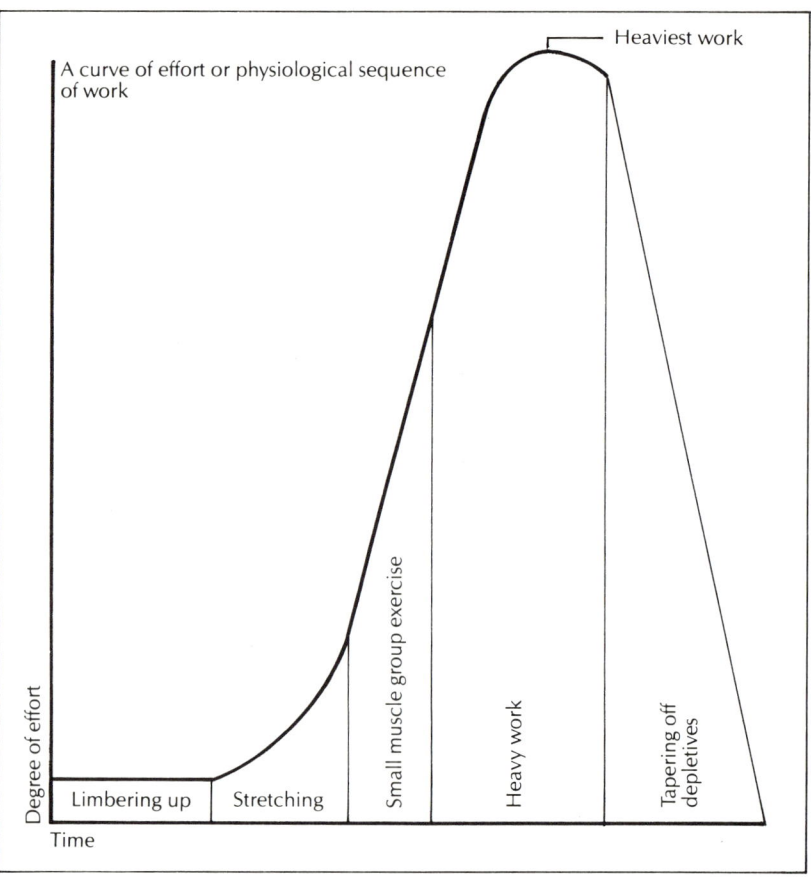

ignore this principle and therefore do not get the most from their routines. I get almost twice as much good out of every repetition as these fellows do because I exercise the muscle on the way up and I am still working it on the way down. Note how in my instructions for the curl (see page 37) I stress that the bar is lowered out and down *under control*. This keeps considerable tension on the arm flexors, giving the biceps and brachialis a lot of extra work. If I ignored this principle, as so many do, the pull of gravity would lower the bar without my needing to employ much muscle work at all. Eccentric work occurs only if you lower the bar more slowly than the speed of gravity. When you straighten the arm *faster* than the speed of gravity — to slap the thigh, for example — then your triceps, a completely different muscle, is working.

Just to complete this short résumé on muscle work, let me mention *static* muscle work, when the muscles work at an unchanging length to hold a fixed position. For example, in a bent-forward rowing motion the muscles of the hips and those at each side of the spine are working statically to hold that position while the arms bend and stretch — while the muscles of the arms and the *upper* back are working concentrically and eccentrically.

A few years ago there was a craze for isometric work. What that short-lived vogue was about was really only static muscle work carried to an advanced degree.

I have quoted this aspect of kinesiology because it is an important principle and because it shows you how much scientific application can be involved in bodybuilding. Take every opportunity to learn about your body and how it works.

## Curve of effort

Training injuries can of course be disastrous if a major event is approaching, but at a lower level even the least competitive bodybuilder wishes to avoid strains and sprains. Some advice is therefore necessary.

The term 'curve of effort' is intended to indicate an accepted approach to workouts whereby there is a gradual increase in the intensity of effort until you are doing the hardest work, near the middle of the schedule; the expenditure of effort then tapers off to the finish. Top sportsmen in the most physically demanding sports use this principle and it is extremely sensible, so you should know how to apply it.

First of all you should spend a few minutes limbering up with simple exercises to loosen the joints and get the blood moving more swiftly through the veins. A few gentle stretching exercises come next, so that when you come to use the weights your joints will be more prepared for the hammering they will inevitably receive in the course of your schedule. When you are young you may not feel the need for such limbering up; however, just like taking out an insurance policy, you'll reap the benefits

# GENERAL INSTRUCTION

later in life, so take heed of this advice.

You will now be ready for your lifting movements. The heaviest movements, those which make you puff and pant, should be included about half to two-thirds of the way through the schedule.

The routine should be finished off with exercises which do not take a great deal out of the heart and lungs; we sometimes refer to these as 'tinkering' exercises. Those exercises for small muscle groups are best done either early or late in the schedule. It is quite important that you do not end with very heavy work and/or stop the workout abruptly. Physiological experts are agreed that depletive work — that is, simpler movements or perhaps even just strolling around — is necessary to allow blood pressure and the pulse to return to normal in the most beneficial manner.

## Foot spacing

In the text for the exercises in Chapter 4 the instruction will often simply state, 'stand with the feet apart', or words to that effect. This is because in all exercises a stable base is required, so in standing exercises — instead of standing with your feet together in military style, as was the case in the past — your feet are placed astride and with the natural turn of the toes. The width of this spacing will depend on your size. If you are tall you will have a wider foot-spacing than a short fellow because, the higher your centre of gravity is, the less stability you are likely to have. As a rule, setting your feet at hip-width apart is a good choice; in this position not only is balance good but the bones of the legs are in a position to support maximum weight.

Those of average height and build should have their heels about 14in (36cm) apart so, depending on your physical structure, adjust your spacing to more or less than this.

## After exercising

Every square inch of the skin contains thousands of small pores which exude impurities, thereby assisting the work of the kidneys, lungs, etc.

Nowadays it is hardly necessary to stress the need for a shower or bath after training, but this was not always so. In our great-grandfathers' day only the more affluent had baths in their homes — we called them 'filthy rich' if they had a couple of baths.

To highlight the changing situation we can recall the tale of the titled lady who asked her new maid to prepare her bath. 'But it isn't Saturday, ma'am,' stuttered the servant, only to be told that the Mistress had a bath daily. '*Every* day?' queried the maid, and with shaking head she departed. 'I don't want to work for a person dirty enough to need baths seven days a week!'

Even in the roughest of training quarters, it should be possible to wash down in order to remove all perspiration before donning a clean set of clothes — *not* those you wore for your workout.

If you are very warm, even if you are the most macho of muscle men you should start the shower with warm water and gradually change to cold. Likewise, no matter how 'fragile' you may be, you should always try to finish with a cool or cold shower and a brisk towelling.

## Relaxation

Rest and relaxation after and between workouts are quite essential. Having showered and towelled you should taper down, relaxing slowly if conditions permit. If, on the other hand, there is only changing space, then you should dress without haste and consciously relax as you do so. Allow every part of your body to relax completely; try to feel the tension flow out of the muscles after their exertions. With practice this can become a very refreshing and invigorating interlude that you will come to enjoy.

There must be adequate rest between workouts so that broken-down tissue can be rebuilt with extra compensation if you are to achieve bodybuilding.

It almost goes without saying that you need adequate sleep to make the most of your workouts — but some young bodybuilders seem committed to burning the candle at both ends. You may have a wonderful light for a short time but, like the candle, you will soon burn out if you indulge in this sort of life-style.

# 4 Bodybuilding exercises

## Arms

When the kids say 'show us your muscles' they do not expect a lat spread, trap over or calf contraction. All they have in mind are flexed biceps.

To the uninitiated, big arms are considered a sign of strength — and there is some basis for this assumption, since those with larger-than-usual arms have usually done hard physical work and become strong as a result.

Bodybuilders everywhere concentrate on developing the arms more than any other part of the body, so it follows that there is a huge variety of arm-building exercises. Because they are very effective, even a little work on the biceps and triceps can quickly increase size and improve shape.

It is not commonly recognised that the triceps adds more size to the arms than does the biceps; moreover, under the biceps lies the brachialis anticus, which also adds considerably to the bulk of the arms. Finally, across the armpits when the muscles are flexed you can see in advanced bodybuilders a muscle known as the coraco brachialis. All of these muscles must be exercised in order to achieve full arm development.

*Barbell curl: starting position with arms straight and, in this case, with hands set just wider apart than shoulder-width*

*Barbell curl: The finished position, showing the wide range of movement which Bill advocates*

# BODYBUILDING EXERCISES

### Arm flexor group

**BARBELL CURL**
The barbell curl is probably the most popular of all arm exercises. You start this movement holding the barbell across your thighs with your hands about shoulder-width apart. Bend your arms to bring the bar up to your neck, but do not swing your body as you move your upper arms.

Complete the movement by lowering your arms in a controlled manner, ensuring that purely arm work is being performed. I like to push the bar out as I lower it, making a wide semicircle on the way down. The bar should be close to your body on the way up but away from your body on the way down.

**EZ BAR CURL**
This exercise is done with a bar which has a number of bends in it, and is sometimes known as an easy-curl bar. Research has shown that, because of the hand positions possible with this apparatus, better results can be obtained than with a straight bar.

Using a palm-up grip on the medium-spaced curves, hold the EZ bar at arms' length against your upper thighs while standing erect with your feet apart. Next, inhale and curl the bar up to your neck using your arm muscles alone to curl the weight, rather than using a body swing. Lower the bar back to the starting position using the same outward path of movement as described for the barbell curl, controlling the movement to make the biceps resist the weight as much as possible.

Barbell curl: Lowering the bar outwards and downwards away from the body

EZ-bar curl: This bar has various bends to allow a diversity of hand positions, and the revolving ends are also of assistance. Note the chin-high lift when using light weights. Even when the weights are heavy Bill lifts high on the neck, and never just to the upper chest, as some bodybuilders do

Standing dumb-bell curl: This shows the finished position, with the palms turned towards the face

Alternate dumb-bell curls: The weights can be curled alternately, so that one is raised while the other is lowered. In this case the palms are forward throughout the movement

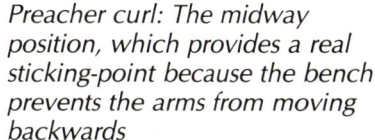
## BODYBUILDING EXERCISES

*Preacher curl: Starting position, with the arms straight and the hands in front of the elbows, which are in turn in front of the shoulders*

*Preacher curl: The midway position, which provides a real sticking-point because the bench prevents the arms from moving backwards*

STANDING DUMB-BELL CURL
Grasp a dumb-bell in each hand, keeping your back straight, head up and feet apart. Curl the dumb-bells up to your shoulders. Your palms should be facing in at the start but, during the curl, turn your palms up when passing the halfway stage and keep them in this position for the remainder of the upward part of the curl. On lowering the weights, turn your palms inwards again before they are fully straightened at your upper thighs.

Inhale as you raise the weights, exhale as you lower.

PREACHER BENCH CURL
This is sometimes called the Scott bench curl, as it was popularised by Larry Scott, the Mormon physique star of the mid-1960s. With palms upwards, grasp a barbell while sitting at a sloping curling bench with your arms against the pad provided. Prevent your upper arms from moving outwards as you curve the bar upwards in a semicircular motion until your forearms and biceps touch. Return to the starting position and repeat, breathing evenly at all times.

*Preacher curl: Finished position, viewed from the front. Again Bill is using an EZ bar, but the same exercise can be done using a straight bar or even a dumb-bell or two*

39

*Preacher curl: If you don't have a preacher bench, use your inner thigh in the same way to hold your upper arm steady*

### CHEATING CURLS

I have my own style of cheating curl which overcomes the major deficiencies of the varieties practised by some other bodybuilders. In my method I give the bar momentum with a heave and hip thrust, using just enough cheat to pass the sticking point which takes place halfway through the curl. This means that my biceps have to work hard in their inner range in order to finish the exercise. The important point comes next: I resist the weight as much as possible as I return the bar to the starting position, lowering the bar as *slowly* as possible. This technique allows me to use much heavier weights than can be used in strict 'military' style. Remember the drill — cheat on the way up and then lower the bar as slowly as possible.

By the way, nowadays I do several kinds of curl during the same workout, but you must take your time before reaching this stage. It's for the very advanced who have done hundreds of bodybuilding training hours.

### Arms extensor group

PUSH DOWN ON PULLEY
This is my favourite exercise and it's a wonderful arm builder. Facing a high wall pulley, grasp the cable handles. Place your feet about one foot (30cm) apart and keep your back straight. Pull the cables down until your upper arms are at your sides. Then, keeping your palms face-down, push your lower arms straight down until your arms are straight and by your sides. Return to the starting position, keeping your upper arms stationary.

FRENCH PRESS OR TRICEPS STRETCH (WITH EZ CURL BAR OR TRICEPS FRAME)
Hold an easy curl bar, dumb-bell or barbell behind your neck, using a close grip. Hold your elbows high; then, keeping the top part of your arms as steady and as close to your head as possible, straighten your arms overhead, locking them firmly at the completion of the movement. As you lower the bar to its original position behind the neck, use the same path. Aim for a full range of movement.

BODYBUILDING EXERCISES

*Push-down on pulley: Starting and finishing positions. The upper arms remain in the same place throughout the exercise*

*Triceps stretch lying: The same exercise, sometimes called a French press, can be done in the standing position. Here Bill is using the EZ bar and employing a close grip*

*Kick-backs: Bill demonstrates the single-arm version of the kick-back, keeping his nonlifting arm on a bench to help maintain good position*

*Triceps dips on chairs: Bill shows here the more advanced version of this exercise, with the feet raised, but the beginner can have his feet on the floor. Make sure that your benches or chairs cannot slip while you're doing the movement*

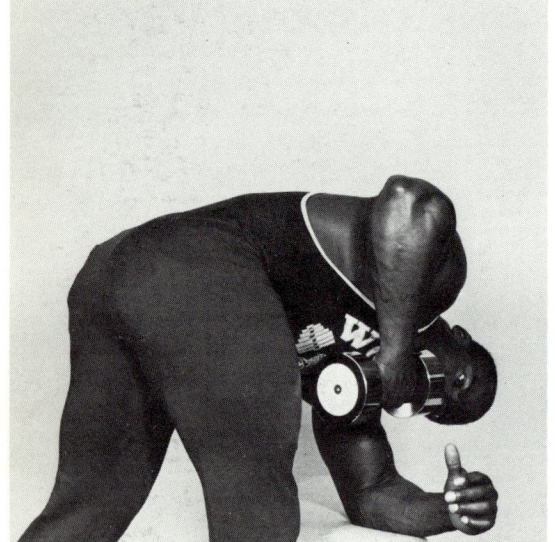

# BODYBUILDING EXERCISES

## KICK-BACKS
Grasp a dumb-bell in each hand with your palms facing down and your body forward. Keeping your arms and body bent, lift your arms backwards and upwards as far as possible. Straighten your arms with a great effort to make a really fierce contraction. Hold the dumb-bells in this position for a short period.

## TRICEPS DIPS ON CHAIRS
Sit between two chairs and place your hands flat on their seats, raising your hips as necessary to bring you into a comfortable position. Your legs should be extended in front of you so that your body is now supported by your feet and hands alone.

You then do press-ups, bending and stretching at the elbow and allowing the hips to rise and fall in order to get a greater range of arm movement. It is very much like doing ordinary press-ups but facing upwards rather than downwards.

## SINGLE-ARM TRICEPS STRETCH WITH DUMB-BELL
Stand erect and grasp a dumb-bell in one hand beside your head; raise the dumb-bell overhead until your arm is straight, keeping the upper arm close to the side of your face. Then lower the dumb-bell straight back and down in a semicircular movement. Keep your upper arm immobile throughout the exercise, bending your arm only at the elbow. Return to the original position, reversing the original movement. Your elbow should point upwards throughout the exercise and, as in all one-arm movements, you should follow with a similar set for the other arm.

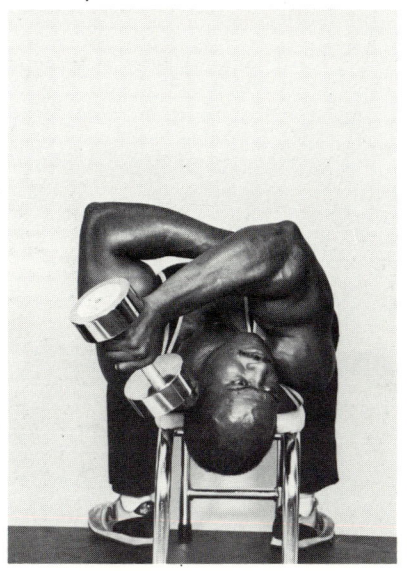

*Lying triceps stretch with dumb-bell: While the standing variation is explained in the text, here Bill shows you how it can be done on a bench. Note, in particular, that the head is over the end of the bench, and look at the position of the nonlifting arm*

## Shoulders

Broad shoulders are very much coveted by young men, whether or not they are physically inclined. Shoulder-width is seen as a sign of virility and athleticism, and wide-shouldered individuals almost invariably look well, regardless of whether they are clothed or not.

Working the deltoids, the muscles which cap the shoulders, will add greatly to your appearance, but it should be noted from the outset that these muscles are split into three parts: the anterior deltoids at the front, the posterior deltoids at the back, and the lateral deltoids at the side. This means that a number of different movements are necessary to give a comprehensive workout. Furthermore, there are several other muscles in this area requiring attention, and of these the trapezius, seen mostly in the 'most muscular' type of pose, deserves special mention.

The exercises in this section ensure that none of these muscles are neglected.

SINGLE-ARM DUMB-BELL PRESS
With one hand lift a dumb-bell to your shoulders and, standing firmly erect, hold the weight with the palm facing inwards and the elbow slightly in. Without any body movement, press the dumb-bell straight up and then return to the starting position. Your free hand may be held sideways to assist balance. Both arms and shoulders should be worked equally.

*Dumb-bell presses: These can be done with one or both hands and with the palm towards the head or facing forwards; the performer can either stand or add to the difficulty by doing the movement while seated. Bill shows here a number of variations*

# BODYBUILDING EXERCISES

### TWO-ARM DUMB-BELL PRESS
This exercise is performed in the same manner as described immediately above, but with a dumb-bell held in each hand. Avoid leaning backwards or using the legs to assist the lift.

### ALTERNATE-ARM DUMB-BELL PRESS
Perform the exercise as described immediately above but, as you lower one arm, begin to press the other arm upwards. When I am doing these presses for the deltoids I do short-range movements and do not lock out the elbows. In other words, I cut out the hardest triceps work from the movements.

### SHORT-RANGE BARBELL PRESS
This is a fine deltoid-builder. With your hands shoulder-width apart, you clean the bar to your chest and adopt a strong and strict pressing position. Without any backbend or heave from the legs, drive the barbell upwards using your shoulder muscles as much as possible. This drive should take the bar well above your head, although personally I make no real attempt fully to straighten the arms. Lower and repeat.

### SEATED DUMB-BELL PRESSES AND COMBINATIONS
The various pressing movements can be done seated as well as standing and, as there is less likelihood of bodily movement in the seated position, I often recommend a special variation of the dumb-bell press. It involves a combination of movements and, although it takes a little while thoroughly to master the sequence, it is worth the effort.

Sit on a bench with a dumb-bell in each hand *but* with your right hand at your shoulder and the left overhead. First press the right dumb-bell until your arm is straight, still holding the left arm straight up. Then, keeping the right arm locked, do a left-arm press. Thirdly, do a two-arm press, both the dumb-bells going up together. This is *not* a see-saw style alternate-press exercise. While one arm is pressing the opposite arm is holding a dumb-bell overhead; this certainly intensifies the exercise. Indeed, I feel that doing 30 reps. this way is worth 70 done by the easier method.

In all dumb-bell presses for the deltoids, I try to lower the weights as much as possible at the shoulders. I concentrate on using these muscles to raise the weights rather than the triceps, which don't matter to me during shoulder workouts.

*Lateral raise with dumb-bells: Midway position*

# BODYBUILDING EXERCISES

*Alternate forward raises with dumb-bells: First one dumb-bell and then the other is raised to above shoulder height*

## LATERAL RAISE WITH DUMB-BELLS

This exercise is excellent for developing the side parts of the deltoids and can be performed standing or sitting. When standing, hold a pair of dumb-bells in the hang position and bend slightly forward from the waist. Then raise the weights sideways and upwards in a semicircular motion, arching your back, until the weights meet overhead. In lateral raises like this it is important to keep the arms sideways in line with the body and not in front of it. I keep my arms nearly straight and allow my wrists to drop as I raise the dumb-bells. In the lying-down version of this exercise, the anterior deltoids and pectorals are strongly used.

## DUMB-BELL UPRIGHT ROWING

With your palms towards you, hold the dumb-bells in front of your thighs; keep your back straight as you bend your arms to raise the weights. Keep the dumb-bells very close to your body and your elbows raised above the weights at all times. The movement is completed when the weights are at chin level and your elbows are pointing straight up. Lower your arms and repeat.

## FORWARD RAISES WITH DUMB-BELLS

Hold the dumb-bells in front of your thighs and lift them forwards and upwards. Your arms should be kept almost straight and your wrists allowed to drop. There are two variations: in one you raise the dumb-bells until they are overhead in a complete semicircle, and in the other version you stop when the weights have passed shoulder-height.

## ALTERNATE FORWARD RAISES

Perform the exercise described immediately above, but raise and lower each arm alternately.

The Ultimate Physique

*Upright rowing: Starting position*

*Upright rowing: Finished position, with the bar right up to above chin-level*

## UPRIGHT ROWING
Hold a barbell in front of your thighs with your hands about four or five inches (10–13cm) apart and your palms towards you. I judge the distance by spreading my thumbs along the bar until they just touch. Keep your body upright and stationary and bend the arms, keeping your elbows out to the sides and raised above the bar at all times. Bring the bar up to just above your chin and pause for a moment. The bar should be kept very close to your body throughout the exercise. Most bodybuilders lift as far as the neck only, but I take the bar above chin level.

## MILITARY PRESS
Clean the weight to your chest and lock your back, legs and hips. Press the weight overhead using your arm and shoulder strength alone. Lower the weight to your upper chest and rest it there for just a fraction of a second before proceeding with the next repetition. Avoid bending your back.

## PRESS BEHIND NECK
Hold the bar behind your neck, using a wider grip than is usual, allowing for comfort. Press the barbell overhead, directing it slightly backwards. Lower the bar until it is as low on the 'traps' as possible and pause before each repetition. This exercise can be performed sitting down, making the press more severe.

## BODYBUILDING EXERCISES

*Military press: Starting position. Bill uses a 'thumbless' grip; that is, with his thumb alongside the fingers instead of around the bar, so that the weight is allowed to be more over the heel of the hand*

*Press behind neck: Starting position, with the bar low on the neck. This picture illustrates the 'thumbs-around' style of grip*

*Military press: The weight is pressed overhead without the body moving from its starting position*

*Press behind neck: Bill, in a raised position, demonstrates the 'thumbless' grip*

## The Ultimate Physique

**FRONT RAISE WITH CABLES**
Stand with your back towards the cable pulley machine, so that there is tension on the handle as you hold it a few inches behind your thigh. Using the strength of your shoulder muscles only, swing your arm forwards and upwards until it is above the level of your shoulder; your arm must be kept straight throughout the movement. Lower your arm and repeat the exercise until you have completed the set.

*Front raise with cables: Starting position. Note the position of the hand, with the palm backwards and the knuckles forwards*

*Front raise with cables: Finished position. The arm, still straight, is raised above shoulder level*

# BODYBUILDING EXERCISES

**LATERAL RAISE WITH CABLES**
Stand sideways to the cable machine, so that your pulling hand is towards the low cable. Lift your arm sideways and upwards until it is in line with your shoulders. In this exercise, unlike the preceding one, you may bend your arm *slightly* to ease the strain on the elbow joint — but don't overdo it. Lower your arm under control, and repeat the movement the required number of times.

*Side (or lateral) raise with cables: Starting position, with the arm straight and the knuckles pointing sideways*

*Side (or lateral) raise with cables: Finished position, with the arm raised until it is in line with the shoulder while the body is maintained in an erect position*

# The Ultimate Physique

## Chest

To develop the chest it is best to concentrate initially on ribcage-expanding exercises, rather than merely developing the external muscles of the chest. So at first exercise with the aim of greatly enlarging the ribcage and then later do more exercises to develop the superficial muscles, such as the pectorals and serratus anterior.

One way to increase the size of the ribcage is by forced breathing. Perhaps surprisingly, leg exercises play an important role in this, because such exercises quickly stimulate respiration and cause breathlessness. To benefit fully from this forced breathing it is ideal to include stretching exercises while you are still breathing deeply between each set of leg movements. When doing lifting exercises to increase chest size, weight is relatively unimportant as it is mobility which you are aiming for rather than poundage.

Leg work is detailed on other pages (see pages 74–81); here we will give attention to exercises which build the muscles of the chest, the eye-catching 'pecs.', as bodybuilders term the pectoralis major.

*Bench press: Different hand spacings are used as the trainee progresses, but as a general rule beginners should use a narrower hand-spacing than their more experienced colleagues*

*Bench press: Lowering the bar to the neck is more difficult than lowering it to the chest. You should always use assistants when you are engaged in top efforts*

BODYBUILDING EXERCISES

*Bench press: Bill demonstrates the collar-to-collar grip, as used by advanced bodybuilders*

BENCH PRESS

Lie on your back on a sturdy bench and place your arms straight and over your face. Have assistants ('spotters') put a loaded barbell into your hands, and make sure you have a good comfortable grip. Initially your hands should be just wider than shoulder-width apart, but the grip can be widened as you gain experience. Some like to take the weight off the stands themselves or at least to assist the spotters.

To perform the bench press, lower the barbell until it touches your chest and then quickly press it back to the starting position. You will very soon be able to use heavier weights and to widen your grip, thus developing the lateral portion of the pectoralis major.

## The Ultimate Physique

**DUMB-BELL BENCH PRESS**
Dumb-bells are harder to control than a barbell, so the pecs. have to work that bit harder in this exercise. Here you concentrate on lowering to the full range, stretching the front deltoids and chest muscles; this is very important. Now, although I get this full lowering, I don't do a full triceps lock-out: I just heave upwards from the low position without fully straightening my arms before I lower and repeat. I use 130lb (59kg) dumb-bells. I feel it is important that I am in total control of both weights at all times, not only as regards the width of my hand-spacing and the depth to which I lower the weights but also in terms of the speed with which I do the exercise.

You should use your mind to dictate the procedure and pace. For example, sometimes I press slowly upwards and lower slowly as well to make sure I'm doing good concentric and eccentric work. At other times, I work my arms like pistons — quickly up and then quickly, but controlledly, down; these fast reps. build power and get to deep-seated muscle fibres.

*Dumb-bell bench press: The starting and finishing positions. At the lowest point in the movement there should be a good stretching of the chest muscles. Bill increases the effort required for the exercise by raising his feet off the floor, but beginners will find that keeping them on the floor increases stability*

BODYBUILDING EXERCISES

DUMB-BELL FLYING EXERCISE
Lie on your back on a bench and hold a dumb-bell in each hand at arm's-length above your face. As you lower the dumb-bells, bend your arms a little and let them travel outwards, going sideways and downwards as far as possible. Return to the starting position following the same path in reverse, still keeping the arms bent. Try to feel the stretch on the chest as you lower the weights, and keep the tension or pressure on the muscles of the chest throughout the exercise.

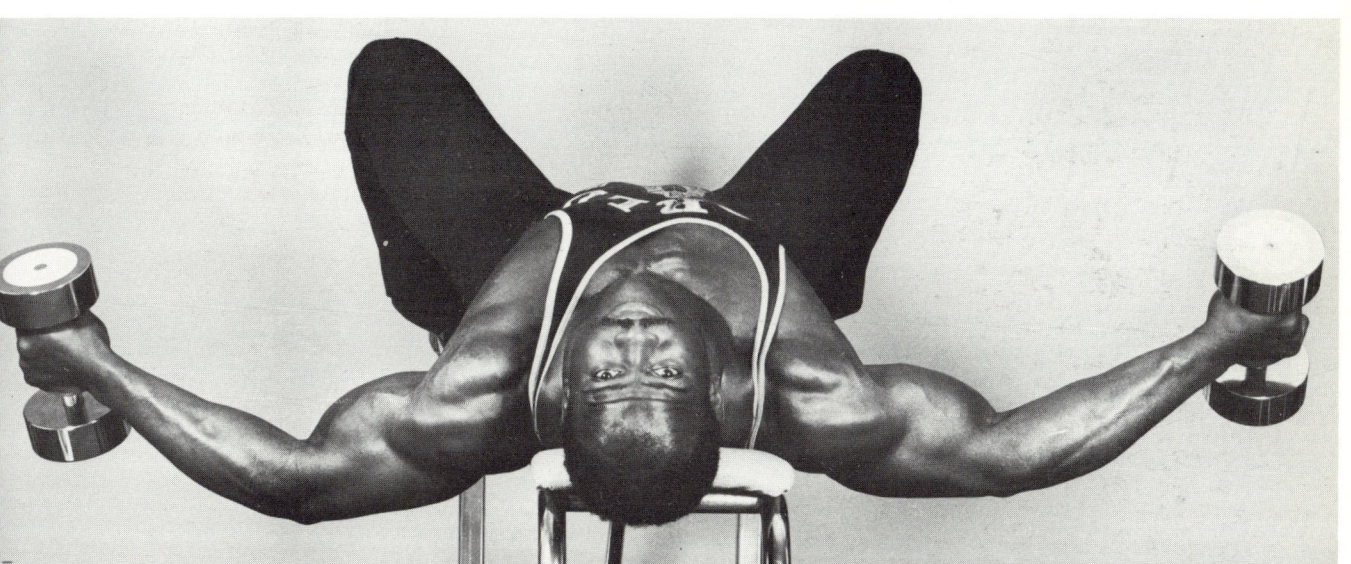

*Dumb-bell flying exercise: The starting and finishing positions. Note how the arms are slightly bent to ease the strain on the elbow joints*

# The Ultimate Physique

*Incline bench work: In exercises of this type the head is higher than the hips; the steeper the angle, the more work is done on the upper pectorals*

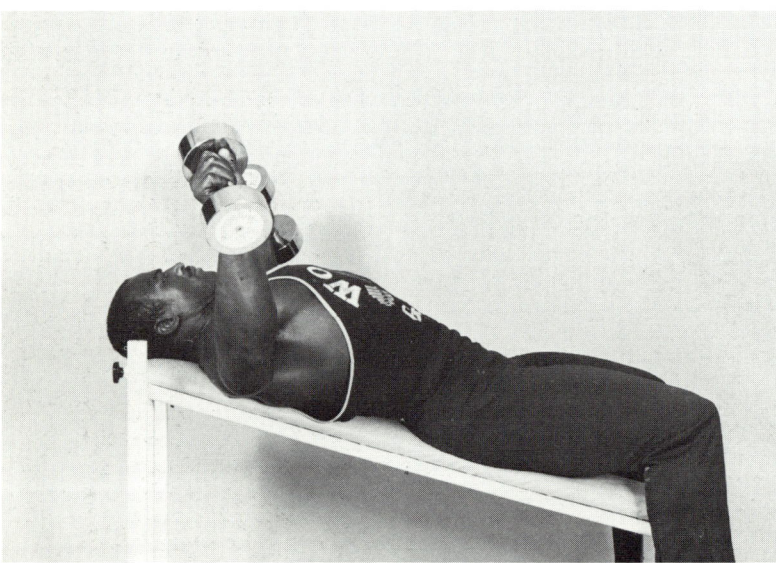

**DUMB-BELL INCLINE PRESS / DUMB-BELL DECLINE PRESS**
You can vary the bench press by adjusting the bench to different angles; either dumb-bells or barbells can be used. Once again, the width of the grip will make a difference to which muscle or section of muscle is being worked the most.

One variation is the *incline bench press*, where you lie with your head to the top of the bench. This exercises the upper pectorals and deltoids. It is important to keep your hips on the bench while pressing the bar overhead.

When performing the *decline bench press*, you lie with your head down and your legs up. In this case, the feet have to be secured, either with a strap or by being held tightly by a training partner. Perform the bench press as described previously, but this time lower the bar to the neck. Decline presses work the lower part of the pectorals.

**PEC DECK**
There are now a number of machines available to add variety and special effects to bodybuilding, but only occasionally do we find something special, whose values and properties compare with those of free weights. The pec deck is one such invention. It has the advantage of being an excellent pectoral builder which allows the user to sit in a comfortable upright position and train the pectorals without

# BODYBUILDING EXERCISES

*Decline bench work: The head is lower than the hips, and the lower pectorals get more of the work*

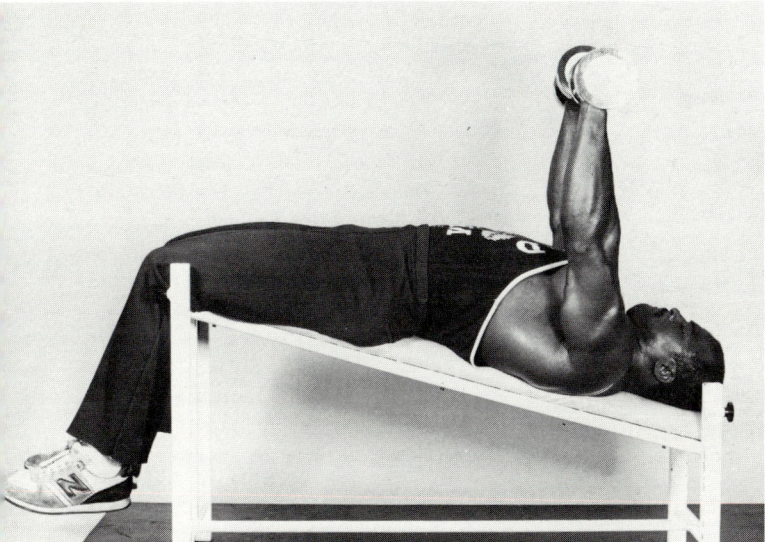

*The pec deck: This is a specialised piece of machinery for exercising the main chest muscles. The resistance is provided by a weight-stack behind and below the performer*

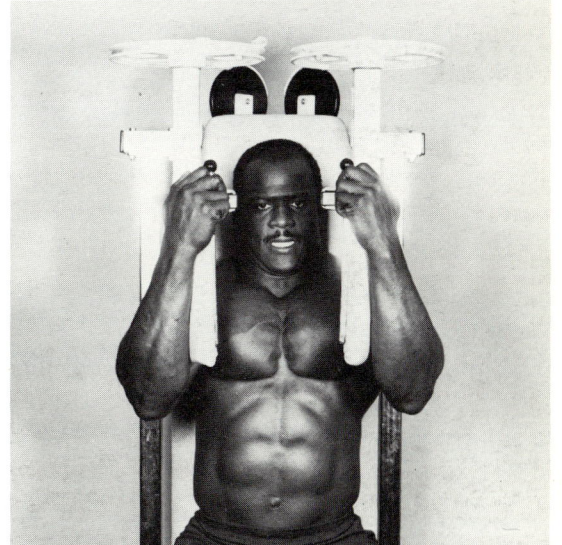

needing any assistants present, as you do for heavy bench work.

The forearms are placed against the pads provided, and the arms are then pulled together in a crushing action, which fiercely contracts the big chest muscles.

The machines are expensive but, if you can find a gym that has one, then be sure to include this sort of work in your schedule.

# The Ultimate Physique

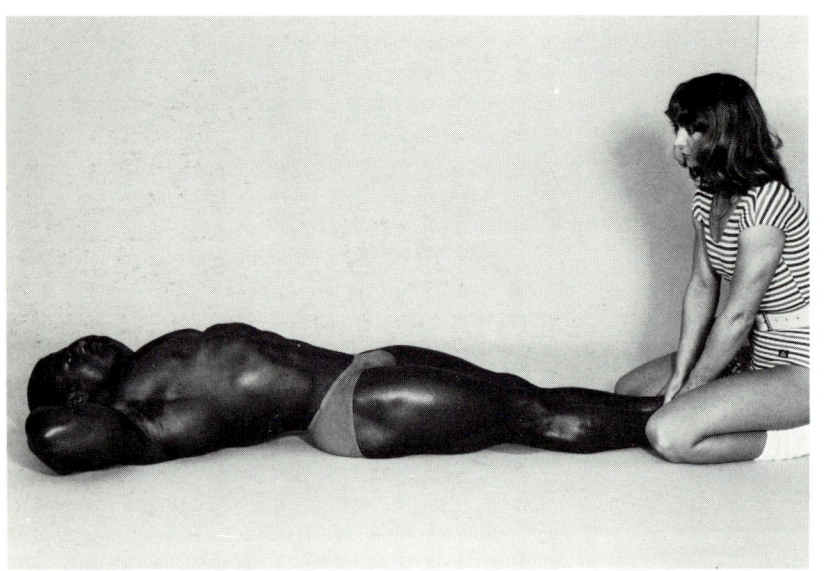

## Abdominals

Very often a person with an excellent physique can fail to develop the abdominal muscles properly, preferring to aim for a very slender waist. However, there are very good reasons for fully developing the abdomen. Firstly, the 'sculptured' look seen in the ancient Greek statues can be very attractive. More importantly, the muscles of the abdomen help to maintain posture; they also have respiratory functions and help protect the abdominal contents by guarding the internal organs from external attacks and by supporting these organs. Finally, if

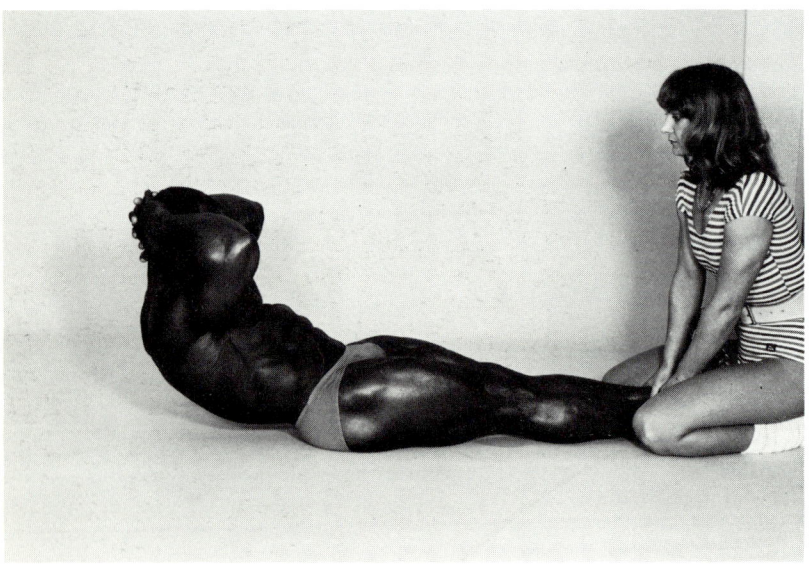

*Straight-leg sit-ups: Three positions during the exercise. It is important to note the way the back is rounded as much as possible before the sit-up continues*

BODYBUILDING EXERCISES

the abdomen is well developed this will prevent those 'bulges' and 'spare tyres' which are so despised.

STRAIGHT-LEG SIT-UPS
This is an exercise with which most people are familiar but often do not perform correctly. Lie flat on your back on the floor with your hands behind your head. Then pull your body upwards, keeping your feet on the floor and making sure you round the back to avoid making the hip flexors do all the work: rounding the back to bring ribs and pelvis closer together is the part of the exercise which contracts the abdominals.

A more difficult variation of this exercise is to perform it as described above but with the feet supported and with weights held behind the neck. To increase difficulty, perform on an inclined abdominal (sit-up) board.

BENT-KNEES SIT-UPS
This exercise is best performed on an adjustable inclined sit-up board. With your feet under the strap at the high end of the board and your knees bent, put your hands behind your head and your chin on your chest. Next lie back until your lower back touches the board, and then return to the starting position, rounding your back as you sit up. The steeper the slope the more difficult the movement. So initially do the exercise flat on the floor and work up gradually.

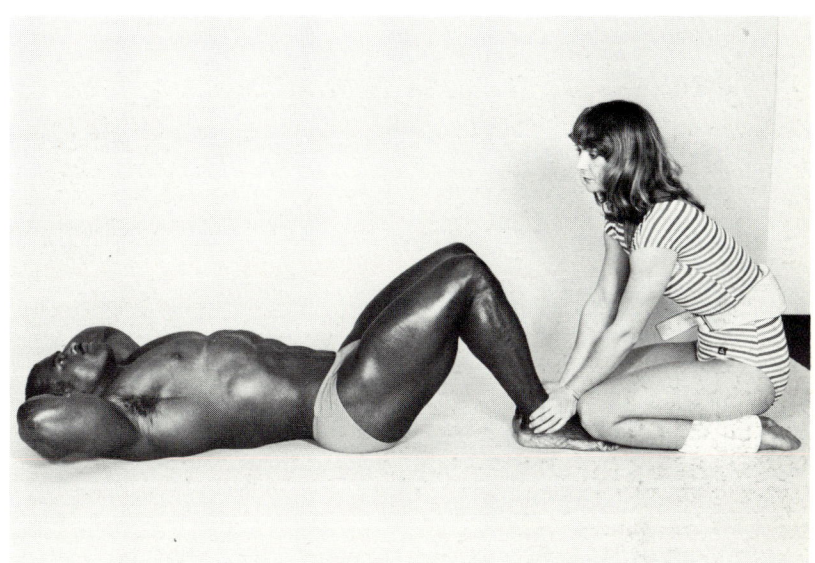

*Bent-knee sit-ups: Although the hamstrings at the back of the thighs are now relaxed, the back is still rounded as much as possible in order fully to contract the abdominal muscles*

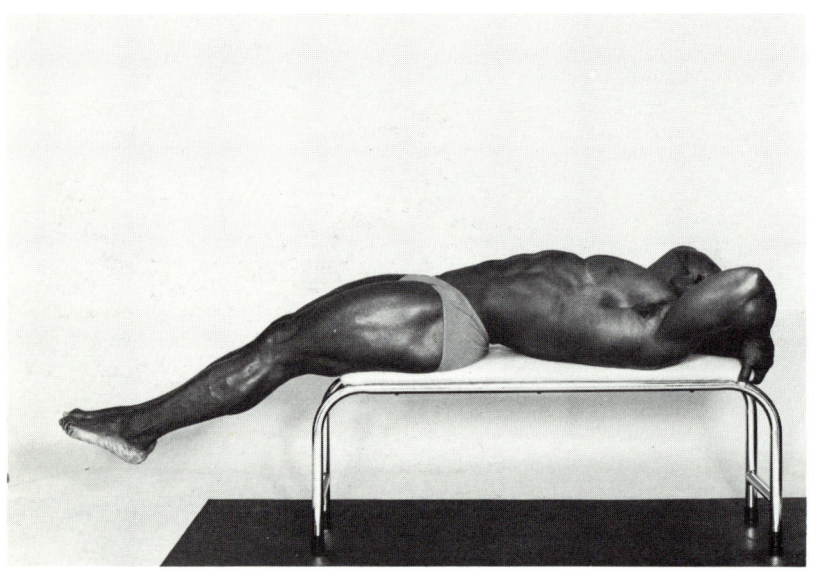

## LEG-RAISES ON TOP OF BENCH OR AT TOP OF STAIRS

Lie back on a bench with your legs over the end and place your hands, palms down, beneath your hips. Then raise your legs as high as possible, keeping your knees locked and your legs straight. At the finishing position your legs should be at a right angle to your torso. I often do sets of these at home, increasing the range of movement by putting my legs over the end of the stairs.

Leg raises on bench: By lying on a bench it is possible to start with your feet below the level of your hips and so allow yourself an increased range of movement

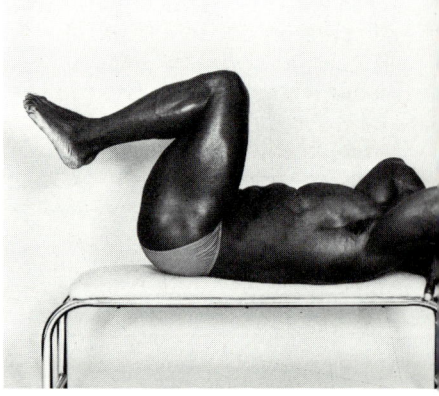

Bent-knee raise: With the hands holding onto the end of the bench, the legs are raised and the knees bent. In order to increase the severity of the exercise and to involve the oblique muscles, the legs can then be lowered first to one side and then to the other

# BODYBUILDING EXERCISES

*Seated twists: As well as the variation described in the text, twists can be done sitting upright and turning from side to side, always pausing in the middle so that the muscles are not assisted by momentum*

## SEATED TWISTS

Perform this exercise in the same manner as the bent-knees sit-up but, instead of sitting straight up, twist your upper body to the right to put your left elbow to your right knee. Return to the starting position and next time twist to the left, putting your right elbow to your right knee. Make each a dynamic twist to exercise the oblique muscles as well as the abdomen.

The Ultimate Physique

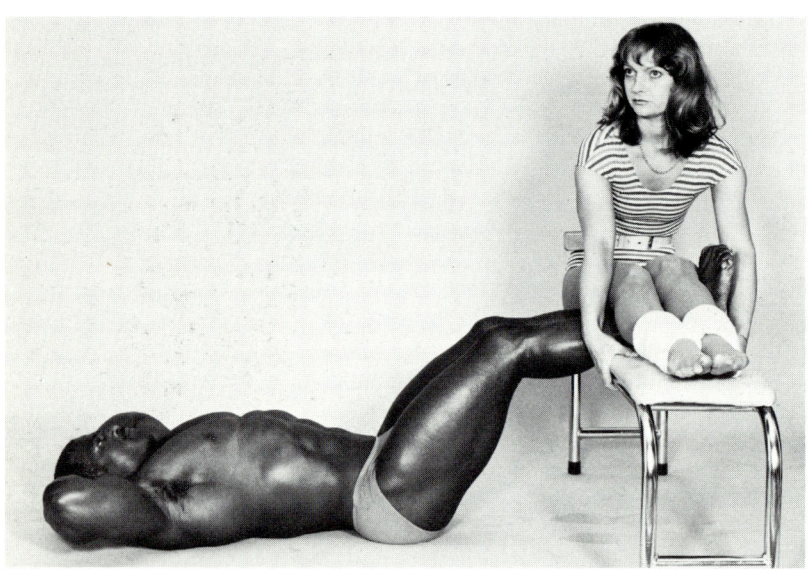

*Squeezes: Here you must 'crunch' the abdominal muscles together, making the distance between your ribs and pelvis as short as possible*

SQUEEZES (CRUNCHES)
Lie on the floor and put your calves over a stool or bench. Now place your hands behind your head and your chin on your chest. Begin to raise your body while twisting it to the right. Sit up as far as possible. Return to the starting position and then sit up straight, to the centre position. Then repeat, but twisting to the left. Carry on this routine, always doing a centre sit-up in between the twists to the right and left.

SIDE-BENDS
Stand up straight with your feet about a foot (30cm) apart, your arms hanging by your sides and a dumb-bell in each hand. Bend to one side as far as possible, and then bend to the other side, keeping your head up and without leaning backwards or forwards. Repeat about ten times to each side.

BODYBUILDING EXERCISES

*Side bends: From the starting position shown, bend as far as you can to the side — but without leaning either forwards or backwards. With a dumb-bell in one hand only, the counterbalancing effect is eliminated*

*Alternate leg raises: Here the leg is being raised prior to being lowered across the body and onto the floor to complete the crossover*

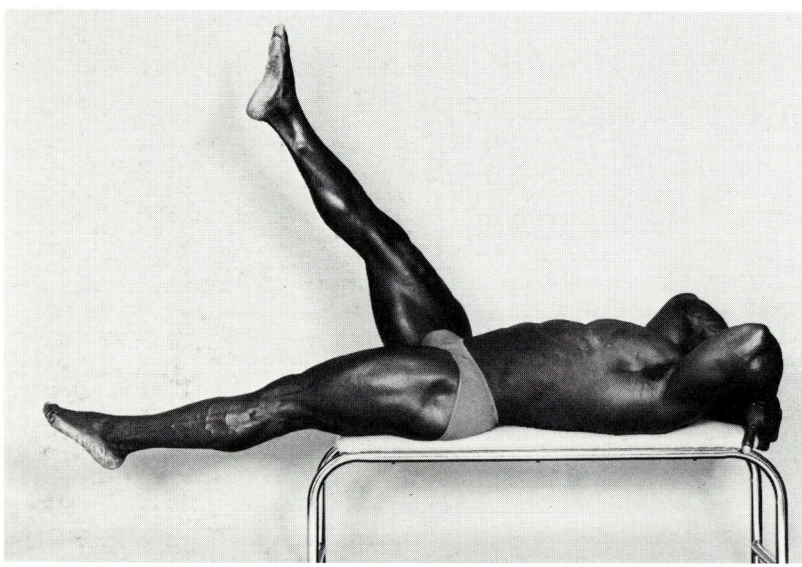

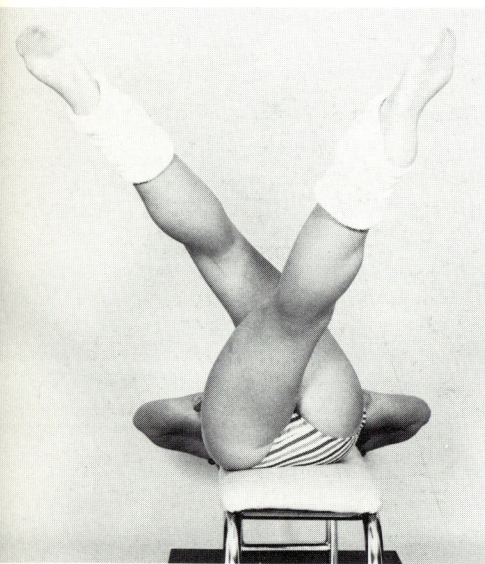

*Crossovers: Another variation, the partial crossover, is demonstrated here. This is particularly popular with women bodybuilders*

### ALTERNATE LEG-RAISING AND CROSS-OVERS

Cross-overs are performed lying on your back, preferably with your hands gripping onto some object behind you. Swing one leg over the other as far as you can, keeping it straight and close to the floor. Return to the starting position and repeat with the other leg. Both your shoulders must stay on the floor throughout the exercise.

Vary this exercise by swinging both legs to one side as far as possible and then repeating the movement to the other side.

### Back

The back is often neglected by bodybuilders. This is a big mistake for, although it is not so easily seen by the individual concerned, the back shows up experience and effort. The more mature bodybuilders usually have good backs because cumulative effort over the years has laid down slabs of muscle at each side of the spine and across the shoulders.

The back is of a rather complicated composition, having approximately 400 muscle attachments, 400 ligaments, 118 joints and 168 processes. One of the reasons for this complexity is that it is necessary for the spine to have not only stability but also great mobility.

Scandinavian physical educators used to believe that development of the back was the essential point in developing the whole physique. There is some truth in this, as good posture is closely linked to the work you do in this region.

The back can be divided into various sections: the upper back, the lower back, and the latissimus dorsi.

Exercises for the upper back give you that well defined muscular appearance and develop those muscles which are important in the acquisition of good posture. The lower back is even more important, because it represents a basic zone of power. The latissimus dorsi are showy muscles which are seen to

# BODYBUILDING EXERCISES

advantage from both front and rear aspects.

It is, therefore, important to do a large variety of carefully chosen exercises, to develop the back fully and correctly.

**Rowing motion**
There are a number of rowing-type exercises using barbells, dumb-bells and pulley weights, all of which affect the back muscles in different ways.

The standard version of the rowing motion using a barbell provides a good example of how the effect of an exercise can be changed. Here is my favourite method of performing this exercise.

My intention is to work the muscles of the upper back — those across the top of the shoulders and between the shoulder blades — which when contracted make the area look like a relief map of the Peak District. I take a very wide hand-spacing as this cuts down on biceps work.

Bending forward from the waist, I push the hips back and bend the knees *slightly* to take the strain off the hamstrings. I fix my eyes on some object in front of me — this helps to keep my torso in the same place as I bend my arms to bring the bar high on my chest between my neck and my nipples. This high position is important because the upper-back muscles do not do nearly so much work if you pull the bar low: pulling the bar to the lower

*Rowing: The starting and finishing positions. Bill favours the wide hand spacing, as shown here, but from time to time he varies the spacing*

chest or waist works the lats, but that is not my aim here.

*Single-arm rowing: A bench is used to cut down on the amount of body movement. The weight is pulled to the lower chest*

### SINGLE-ARM ROWING

Although the term 'rowing' is used, this movement involves a sort of sawing rather than rowing motion. A dumb-bell is placed on the floor in front of a bench. You bend down and place your right hand on the bench to give support and to keep your upper body steady. Then you lift the dumb-bell just a few inches from the floor. Next, raise the dumb-bell straight up to your chest with a long pulling movement, bending your arm and keeping it close to your body.

Repeat the same number of movements to each side, remembering not to allow the weight to touch the floor once you have begun. It helps if you put to the rear the leg corresponding to the lifting arm; i.e., left leg back when lifting with the left hand, and vice versa.

I do all my sets for one side before I work the other side, rather than working left and right alternately.

### SINGLE-END ROWING

These rowing exercises give good latissimus and upper-back development. One variation is to use a barbell loaded at one end only, anchoring the unloaded end to the foot of a wall or to the floor using a loop or immoveable object. First, stand astride the bar with your back towards the empty end, holding the loaded end. Then lift the weight in the usual rowing motion. The close grip and more upright stance gives quite a change of muscle

# BODYBUILDING EXERCISES

*Lat pulley: The illustration on the left shows the starting position and the other two the most popular variations of this exercise: pulling to the chest, and pulling to behind the neck*

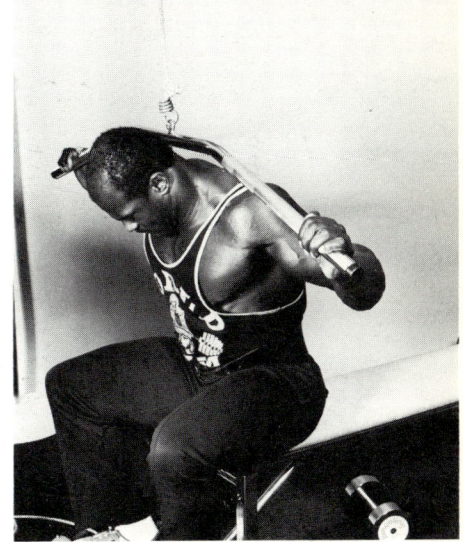

work. The use of a T-rowing bar considerably enhances the exercise.

With the barbell loaded at only one end you can also perform single-arm rowing. To do this you have the bar at right-angles to your front and hold the bar just by the inside collar, so that at the end of the lift the position of your rowing arm is very similar to the one adopted at the end of the standard variation of the rowing motion.

To help keep your body still and to avoid unnecessary movement during this lift, your free hand should be placed on the corresponding knee. These movements will help you to get the 'V-taper' effect coveted by so many people and, as a good lat spread is a real eye-catcher, the exercises should be a regular part of your schedule.

**Lat pulley pull-downs**
Kneel in front of a lat machine and, with your arms extended overhead, place your hands wide apart on the lat pulley bar. Pull the bar down until it reaches your upper chest. Return to starting position and repeat.

This exercise can also be done pulling to the back of your neck and shoulders. I do four sets of 10-12 reps. to the back and then, without pause, the same again but pulling to the chest.

ALTERNATE SINGLE-ARM PULL-DOWNS TO BACK OF NECK
Perform this exercise in the same manner as the previous one, but pull the bar down behind your head to the back of your neck. I do single-arm pull-downs to the front as well, and sometimes superset these two related exercises.

The Ultimate Physique

*Pulley-rowing with high pulley: Get a good stretch before you start the pull, then raise your head as you begin it and take the bar right down to your chest*

BODYBUILDING EXERCISES

### PULLEY-ROWING WITH HIGH PULLEY
If possible, attach a close grip to the high pulley. Sit back from the pulley so that the weights are raised when you grasp the bar with the palms-facing grip. Pull the bar in to your upper chest, with your arms close to your sides. Throughout this exercise you must keep your back straight and your head up.

### PULLEY-ROWING WITH LOW PULLEY
Using a low pulley, grip the pulley handles with both hands. Stand far enough back to allow yourself to support the weight-stacks when you bend from the waist. Pull the cables up to the sides of your chest without bending forward or backward. Return to the starting position.

*Pulley-rowing with low pulley: The starting and finishing positions. This exercise can also be done standing up*

# The Ultimate Physique

Lat stretch pull-down, standing. The first part of the exercise, getting the stretch, is of considerable importance. In the finished position which Bill demonstrates here he has pulled to the lowest point; often the p[ull] is done only as far as the thighs.

# BODYBUILDING EXERCISES

*Hyperextensions: With his thighs supported and his ankles held down, Bill raises his torso while holding the weight behind his head*

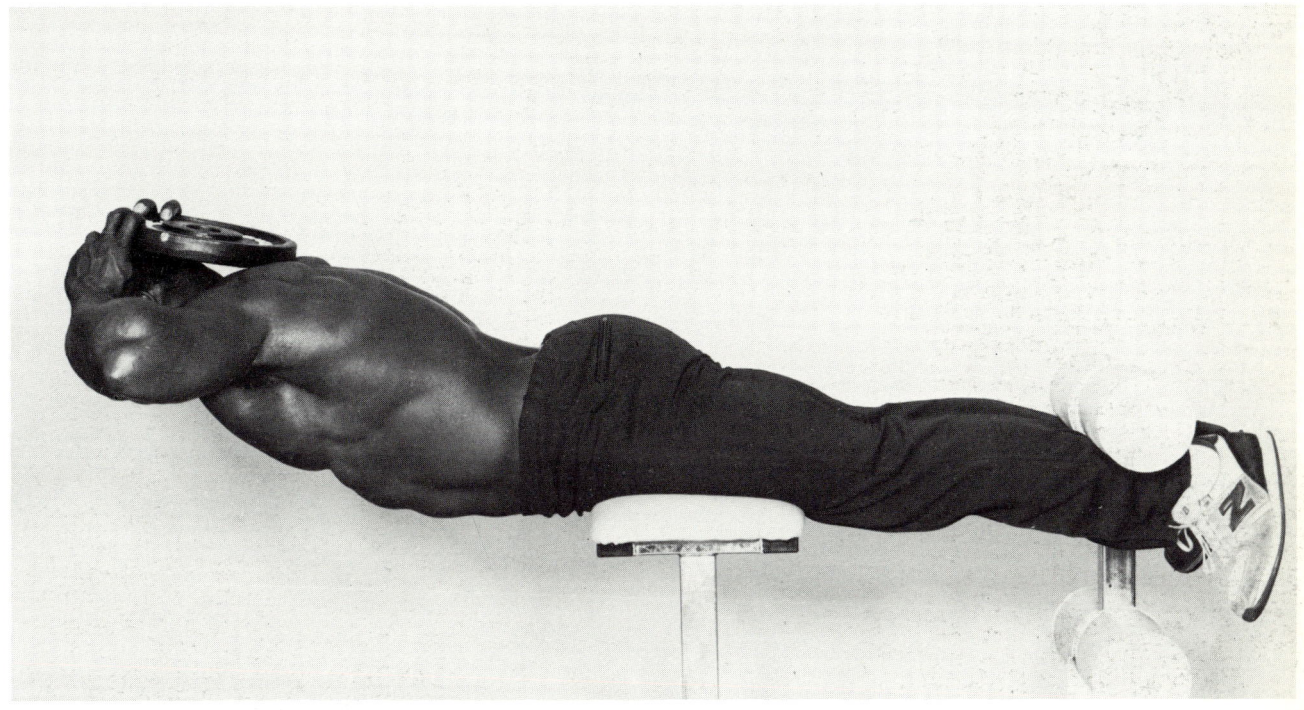

## LAT-STRETCH PULL-DOWN, STANDING

Attach a triangular or short bar to the end of the cable of a high-wall pulley. Grasp the bar with both hands and, keeping your arms straight and knees slightly bent, bend forward from the waist and pull the bar straight down to your thighs. Your arms and back should be kept straight throughout the exercise.

In all of these pulling movements you should concentrate on using the back muscles to execute the action rather than make the arms do most of the work.

## HYPEREXTENSIONS

Beginners should do this exercise.

Without weights and without a bench, lie face-down on the floor. Clasp your hands behind your neck and then lift your head and shoulders as high as possible. Return to the starting position and repeat in sets of eight to ten reps.

In a more advanced form you do hyperextension on a bench either with or without weights. If you have a training partner to hold your ankles, this exercise can be done over the edge of a bench or table, so that you can round your back very much more when in the starting position; your legs and lower hips are supported on the bench and the rest of your body is extended over the end of the bench. The exercise consists of arching your back by raising your head and shoulders as high as you can.

These hyperextensions are often done with discs behind the neck, but this is a very tough advanced exercise.

# The Ultimate Physique

*Dead lift: In the bodybuilding version of this exercise the back is rounded and the legs slightly bent at the start; at the finish the body is brought upright and the back straightened. Note the alternate grasp, with one hand facing forwards and the other backwards*

# BODYBUILDING EXERCISES

*Stiff-leg dead lift: As we can see in these photographs, the back does most of the work, rather than the legs. At the finish the body should be quite erect*

## DEAD LIFTS

These lifts are good for the trapezius and the erector muscles at each side of the spine.

One form of the dead lift is to grasp the bar with your knuckles forward, your arms straight and your legs bent. Next, with your feet at hip-width apart, straighten your legs and stand erect. This brings you into the hang position, and from there you lower the weight and prepare for the next repetition. Very heavy weights can be handled, and the exercise builds great all-round strength.

A great improvement when you are able to use very heavy weights is to use a different grasp, in which you have one hand each way. Straps can be used to assist your grip in maximum efforts.

Another variation for beginners is to perform this exercise with straight legs, bending forward with a rounded back. You straighten up by flattening the bottom part of the spine first, then the middle and finally the top, carrying the shoulders back to finish the movement. Reverse the process as you lower the weight. This rounding of the back makes the erector spinae work in addition to the hip extensors.

## GOOD MORNING

Hold a barbell across your shoulders, as for squatting, with a grip that feels comfortable. Place your feet apart. Bend forward from the waist, keeping your back straight and your head up. As you do this, unlock your knees just a little and bend forward until your torso is almost parallel to the floor, counterbalancing by easing the hips back. Return to the starting position by straightening your back and then gradually straightening your knees. Round the back each time: if you don't, this becomes more of a hip exercise.

This exercise gives you a great repertoire of movements for the back. Stick with them and the results will soon show, giving you a look of strength and the ability to match your appearance.

The Ultimate Physique

## Legs

Nowadays legs get less natural exercise than in past ages, thanks to the increasing use of cars in preference to walking and also because of automatic machinery, which does heavy work previously done by human effort. However, the legs respond very well to progressive exercise, and a great deal of work can be done to improve this area without using up too much time and effort.

Although squats and other such leg movements are high-poundage lifts, fine results can also be achieved with a variety of low-poundage movements. Both heavy weights and light weights should be used for leg work.

There is a strong association between leg work and chest work (see page 52), and many leg movements also become associated with hip and back work. This combination can produce and sustain more work than any other group in the human body.

## Thighs

The muscles at the front of the thigh are extensors of the leg; the four major muscles as a group are called the *quadriceps*. The longest muscle of the body is the *sartorius*, which crosses the thigh diagonally. On the back of the thigh there is the flexor group, consisting of the biceps femoris, semitendinosus and semimembranosus.

THE SQUAT
The squat, or deep-knee bend, is a very familiar exercise to all experienced bodybuilders; some remarkable results can be obtained by practising this one exercise, of which there are several variations.

Throughout the following examples it is important to remember to keep the head up and back straight, and to try not to lean too far forward. Usually the toes and knees point slightly outwards, but various positions can alter the effect on the muscles. However, in order to avoid knee injury, the knees and toes should always be angled in the same direction. The standard version of the squat is done as follows:

Place a weight behind your neck, across the top of your shoulders. Grip the bar, spacing your hands in the position which feels most comfortable. Your feet should be placed firmly, a little wider than hip-width, flat on the floor. Inhale and squat down until the tops of your thighs are parallel to the floor. When this position is reached, restraighten your legs without any pause. Return to the starting position and exhale.

The above exercise can also be done in exactly the same manner but with the feet in a medium stance, placed about 16 inches (40cm) apart.

A final example of a variation of the squat is to have your heels elevated, keeping your back very upright. This exercise is performed as above, with the feet about 16 inches (40cm) apart, but in this case the heels are placed on a plank of wood measuring 2in × 4in (5cm × 10cm). This method of squatting is very good for

## BODYBUILDING EXERCISES

*The deep knee bend, or squat: Bill 'spots' for the demonstrator, who shows two different ways in which to hold the bar; note that you do* not *change your grasp* during *the exercise. It is always advisable to use an assistant when squatting*

*Leg extension: The starting and finishing positions*

developing the upper thighs.

I like doing full squats in pyramid fashion — for example, 5-4-3-2-1 — and can in this way work up to 600lb (272kg).

LEG EXTENSION
One form of this exercise for the lower thighs is begun by sitting on a bench, in the usual manner, at the end of a leg-extension machine. Place the top part of your ankles and feet under the lower foot pads and then position yourself so that the end of the seat is kept against the backs of your knees; place your hands on the bench behind your buttocks, gripping the bench. Inhale and then, without any movement apart from that which takes place at the knee joints, straighten your legs, raising the weights or weight stack until your legs are parallel with the floor. Return to the starting position and exhale.

If you find you tend to 'kick' up or spread your legs, then fasten a lifting belt around your thighs to prevent this.

I do up to 25 reps. with maximum weights.

*Leg curls: These are done on the same machine as in the preceding illustrations. If you look closely you will see that a cable runs to the lower bar; this cable transmits resistance from a weight stack. In other, similar machines disc weights are used to provide the resistance*

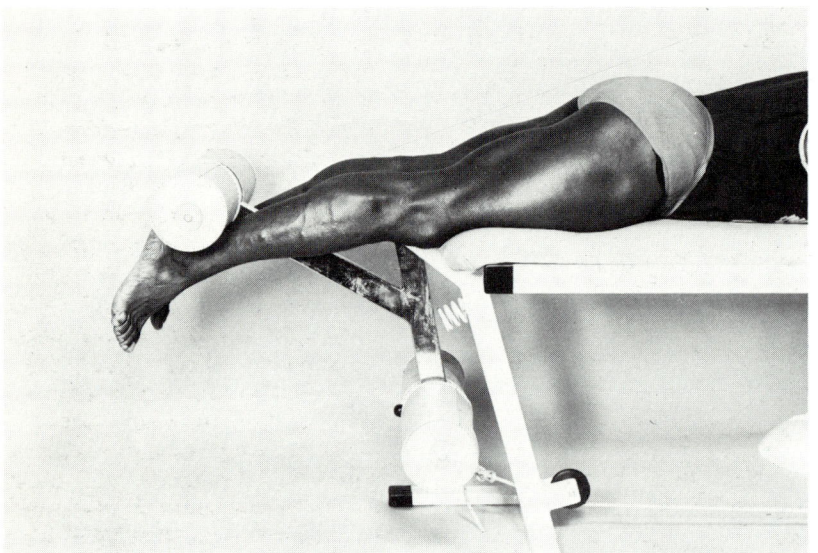

## LEG CURLS

The leg-extension machine can be used also for practising curls. A simple method is to lie face-down on the machine. Straighten your legs and place your heels under the top pads, while gripping the front of the bench. Breathe in and curl your legs up until your lower and upper legs meet. Return to the starting position and exhale. Place a pad under the lower thighs for added range of movement; this also helps resist the tendency to raise your buttocks as you curl.

I always do four sets of these.

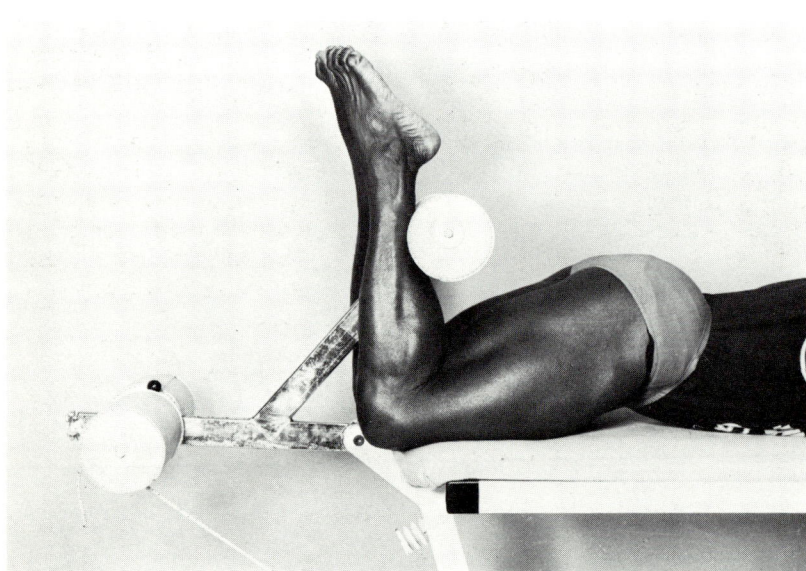

BODYBUILDING EXERCISES

*Hack squats: Here we see the more difficult variation, using free weights as opposed to a machine. This is the position midway between the starting position and the lowest point*

### HACK SQUATS

This exercise was named after George Hackenschmidt, the World Champion wrestler who invented it. It should preferably be performed using a special hack machine, but it can be done with free weights. Not all hack machines are well designed: some seem intended to break your back or cause a hernia!

If using the machine, you step back into it and place your shoulders on the pads, keeping your head up and your back straight throughout. Place your feet about 12 inches (30cm) apart on the slanted platform. Release the safety stops with both hands, then inhale and squat down until your upper thighs are half way to being parallel with the machine. Return to the starting position and exhale.

When doing the exercise with free weights, you hold a barbell behind your back and, keeping your back as upright as possible, you bend and stretch your legs. Push your pelvis forward as you come up.

The Ultimate Physique

LEG PRESSES
This is a fine exercise for the thigh muscles and is done using a wall-type leg-press machine. You simply lie on your back with your hips directly under the foot pad, placing your feet about 12 inches (30cm) apart on the pad. Push the weight rack upwards until your legs are completely straight. Then place your hands, palms downwards, under your buttocks. Inhale and bend your legs to lower the weight rack until your thighs touch the sides of your torso, with the knees slightly out at the sides. Return to the starting position and exhale. A pad under the hips is even more comfortable than your hands, and a slanting support board is often used.

These leg exercises not only enhance your appearance but build up your general health and stamina. Cardiovascular endurance — that is, fitness of the heart and lungs — is a truly valuable commodity which will stand you in good stead throughout your life. That is a wonderful bonus to receive as a result of your bodybuilding training.

*Leg press: The starting and finishing positions. There are several different types of leg-press machine, some involving the use of vertical lifts and others requiring horizontal presses. The incline press shown here falls midway between these two extremes*

*Donkey heel raises: Finishing position. By fixing his upper body with the aid of the bench, Bill is able to concentrate work on the calves. A partner provides the weight resistance in this exercise*

## Calves

At the back of the calf lies the gastrocnemius and under it the soleus; on the front of the lower leg is the tibialis anticus. These muscles are among the most neglected by bodybuilders.

Nearly all the movements involved in calf exercises consist of rising onto the toes and extending the foot. However, the calf muscles are generally considered to be a difficult group to develop, so when performing these exercises it is important to ensure that the lower leg muscles are being fully contracted: they should be worked through the widest possible range.

Having the toes on a block helps increase the range — and I have a very special hint. Get a *narrow* board about 1½in (4cm) wide and 2in (5cm) high so that you can rise right onto the balls of your feet and curl your toes over the edge of the board — those 4in-wide (10cm-wide) boards are not nearly as good.

Get your heels right down in every repetition so that you are working through the widest possible range, from low-heel to high-heel each time.

Calf muscles are high-rep. muscles: they will not grow if you just use heavy weights and low numbers of repetitions. They are in many cases the most difficult muscles to build and, when they prove stubborn, everyday training is sometimes required.

### DONKEY HEEL-RAISES

This is probably the most popular overall calf exercise. Place your toes on a raised block and keep your legs straight throughout; normally you will rest your hands on a bench about a yard (90cm) in front of you. A training partner should now sit on your lower back, staying as still as possible. You should then inhale, rise up onto your toes as high as you can, and hold this position for a moment before returning to the starting position.

As progressive resistance is necessary, it is beneficial if you have a partner whose bodyweight is increasing. Alternatively, of course, use progressively heavier partners.

The angle of the toes and heels will affect which calf muscle is being worked the most. For example, if you turn your toes out and your heels in this will mean that the exercise is affecting the inner calf more, and vice versa.

## The Ultimate Physique

### CALF MACHINE

You can also develop the calf muscles by using a wall calf machine. Firstly, position your shoulders under the extended portion of the machine. Stand straight, and place the balls of your feet on the foot pad below. Keeping your back straight, your head up and your legs locked throughout the exercise, lower your heels as far as possible, then rise up on your toes as high as possible. Hold this position for a second and then repeat.

*Calf machine: Here a free-standing or a wall-fitted calf machine is used for the standing heel raise. In the low position the calves are fully stretched and then, in the raised position, fully contracted*

# BODYBUILDING EXERCISES

*Seated heel raise: The starting and finishing positions*

## SEATED CALF MACHINE

A variation of the previous exercise can be performed seated. Sit on the bench, facing the weights, and place your upper knees and thighs under the pad; then place the balls of your feet on the raised platform. Press the pad up, and then lower your feet to the lowest possible comfortable position. Next rise up on your toes as high as you can, holding the position for a short period. Once again, the position of your toes and heels will influence which part of the calf muscles is being most affected.

In seated heel-raises the soleus receives more work than the gastrocnemius which lies on top of it.

The Ultimate Physique

## 5   Workout routines

In this section, we give some sample routines which will provide a comprehensive scheme of work to someone starting out on bodybuilding or getting back into shape after a lay-off. Advanced enthusiasts are frequently asked to draft routines for others at various stages of training; they could save a good deal of work for themselves by referring future enquirers to this section.

### Beginners' schedule

The worst possible thing for a beginner would be to try to copy the routine of a champion, even with scaled-down weights and scaled-down reps. The needs of novices are entirely different and here are my guidelines for them:

○ Select about ten or a dozen basic exercises, covering all major muscle groups.
○ Use exercises which require movements in more than one joint; e.g., a press instead of a triceps stretch, or a squat instead of leg extensions.
○ Do all exercises with a standard barbell.
○ Have three workouts each week with a rest day between exercising sessions.

### Schedule
○ Warm up with free stretching, etc.
○ Light cleans to shoulder
○ Curl
○ Press
○ Rowing motion
○ Squat with heels on block
○ Bench press
○ Stiff-legged dead lift
○ Pullover at arms-length
○ Sit ups
○ Heel raising

*Week 1*   Each movement ten times with weights well within capacity.
*Week 2*   Twelve repetitions in each exercise.
*Week 3*   Try to add weights in at least half of these exercises.

# WORKOUT ROUTINES

*Week 4*    Add weights in remainder of exercises.
*Week 5*    Fifteen repetitions each exercise.
*Week 6*    Introduce group system — i.e., do each exercise two sets of ten reps.

## Intermediate schedule

The basis of all intermediate training is the proper utilisation of the group system. At this stage, you should introduce some isolated exercises, moving in one joint only. Sets and reps. should be increased. With this schedule you will still be working all muscle groups on the same day. Barbells, dumb-bells and other types of bar can be used, and different apparatus too, if you train in a gym but assuming you are a home trainer here is a routine with free weights:

- Warm up all joints
- Heave jerks (using legs and back as well as arms and shoulders)
- Upright rowing: 2 sets of 10 reps.
- Triceps stretch: 3 sets of 12 reps.
- Dumb-bells curls: 3 sets of 12 reps.
- Incline bench press: 3 sets of 12 reps.
- Front squat: 3 sets of 12 reps.
- Dead lifts: 3 sets of 12 reps.
- Twisting sit-ups: 2 sets of 20 reps.
- Donkey heel-raises: 2 sets of 15 reps.

## Semi-advanced schedules

You are now at the stage of split workouts and, if you intend to go higher, you must train four or five times each week. Schedules A and B should be used alternately, working certain body parts on days 1 and 3 and others on days 2 and 4. You must now do more than one exercise for each body part.

### Schedule A
- Warm up
- Lateral raise standing: 3 sets of 15 reps.
- Press behind neck: 3 sets of 15 reps.
- Pull down on lat pulley: 3 sets of 15 reps.
    *or* Pull ups on chinning bar: 3 sets of 15 reps.
- Rowing motion: 3 sets of 15 reps.
- Good morning exercise: 3 sets of 12 reps.
- Hyperextensions: 3 sets of 12 reps.
- Bench press: 3 sets of 15 reps.
- Decline bench press: 3 sets of 15 reps.
- Flying exercise: 3 sets of 15 reps.

### Schedule B
- Warm up
- EZ bar curl: 3 sets of 15 reps.
- Screw curl with dumb-bells: 3 sets of 15 reps.
- Triceps kickbacks: 3 sets of 15 reps.
- Triceps dips on chairs: 3 sets of 15 reps.
- Leg presses: 3 sets of 20 reps.
- Hack squats: 3 sets of 20 reps.
- Calf machine: 4 sets of 15 reps.
- Seated calf machine: 4 sets of 15 reps.
- Side bends: 3 sets of 20 reps.
- Leg raises: 3 sets of 20 reps.

## Advanced routines

At this stage it is important to work on your weaknesses, as you will probably require special workouts for calves, arms, legs, chest, etc.

### Calf specialisation

I deliberately start this section with calves as they are probably the area in which most specialisation is required; and, as I have always stressed that it isn't what you do but the way that you do it, I will reiterate the requirements for getting results in calf workouts. If calves are your highest priority then begin your workout with these exercises. Work the muscles from every angle in the various movements listed by rising on the toes sometimes with your feet turned in, sometimes turned out and sometimes straight forward. Stand on a narrow strip of wood to raise the toes and thus increase the range of movement. Use the widest range possible, getting a very good stretch when the heels are in the lowest position. Low reps. with heavy weights are out. Never do less than 15 reps. per set but usually 25–30 will be about right, using moderate weights which will allow a good stretch and a good extension of the ankle to get high on the toes. Work the calves at least three times a week and preferably five or six times a week if you are under par.

CALF SCHEDULE AS PART OF A LONGER WORKOUT
○ Standing calf machine:
   3 sets of 30 reps.
○ Seated calf machine:
   3 sets of 30 reps.
○ Donkey heel-raise:
   1 set toes in, 1 set toes out, 1 set toes forward, all with 25 reps.

*Make the calves 'burn' with every set.* Try this routine and you'll soon find out what I mean by the term 'burn'. When you first experience this feeling, remember what it's like and how you achieved it, and then repeat that in every subsequent workout trying to get the feeling by the end of every set.

**Biceps workout**
The front of the upper arm should be full and thick and, when flexed, should swell on top to make an extra peak. The whole area should be well defined, showing clearly the brachialis under the biceps. The following routine should develop even the most obstinate arms. I shall mention the very specific purpose of each exercise to show how there can be specialisation within specialisation! I can't stress often enough that, if you know what you are doing, bodybuilding can be a very exact science.

○ Barbell curls:
   3 sets of 20 reps. for overall mass
○ Preacher bench curls:
   4 sets of 15 reps. for lower biceps
○ Dumb-bell concentration curls:
   3 sets of 15 reps. for biceps peak
○ Reverse curls (palms down):
   3 sets of 15 reps. for tying biceps in with forearms

**Back specialisation**
Pursuing the theme of specialisation within specialisation, I don't just train my back: I think of it in various components. For example, the work of the lower back (erector spinae) has nothing in common with what I do for the lats, and what I do for the lats and the lower back is quite different from what I do for the trapeziuses.

As if that isn't enough, I train the lats in two different ways, with one kind of exercise for adding width and another for adding thickness to the lats. Very few, if any, have ever expounded on this detailed approach to development — there are still a few secrets left among the champions.

**Back routines**
UPPER BACK
○ Trapezius: 3 sets of 20 reps.
○ Shrugs: 3 sets of 20 reps.
○ Cleans: 2 sets of 10 reps.

LOWER BACK
○ Hyperextensions:
   2 sets of 20 reps.
○ Good morning exercise:
   3 sets of 20 reps.
○ Dead lifts: 3 sets of 15 reps.

LATS
○ Chins behind neck:
   4 sets of 10 reps.
○ Low pulley rowing:
   4 sets of 20 reps.
○ Single-arms dumb-bell rowing:
   3 sets of 20 reps. each arm.

**Leg workout**
Really heavy work can be done by the thigh muscles as they are often assisted by the large and strong muscles of the hips. However, I feel that for full development and shape it is necessary also to include some movements in which there is more isolation of the muscle work. This is illustrated in the following very effective leg workout.

○ Squats: 3 sets of 25 reps.
○ Leg extensions: 3 sets of 20 reps.
○ Leg presses: 3 sets of 20 reps.
○ Leg curls: 3 sets of 15 – 20 reps.

**Chest work**
I have left what is probably my best body-part to the last, and what I have to say in this context may surprise many experienced bodybuilders. A very high percentage of enthusiasts have too narrow vision when it comes to chest work. While I have derived great benefit from the bench press, the standard variation is overworked and there should be much more variety in the chest workouts of most

# WORKOUT ROUTINES

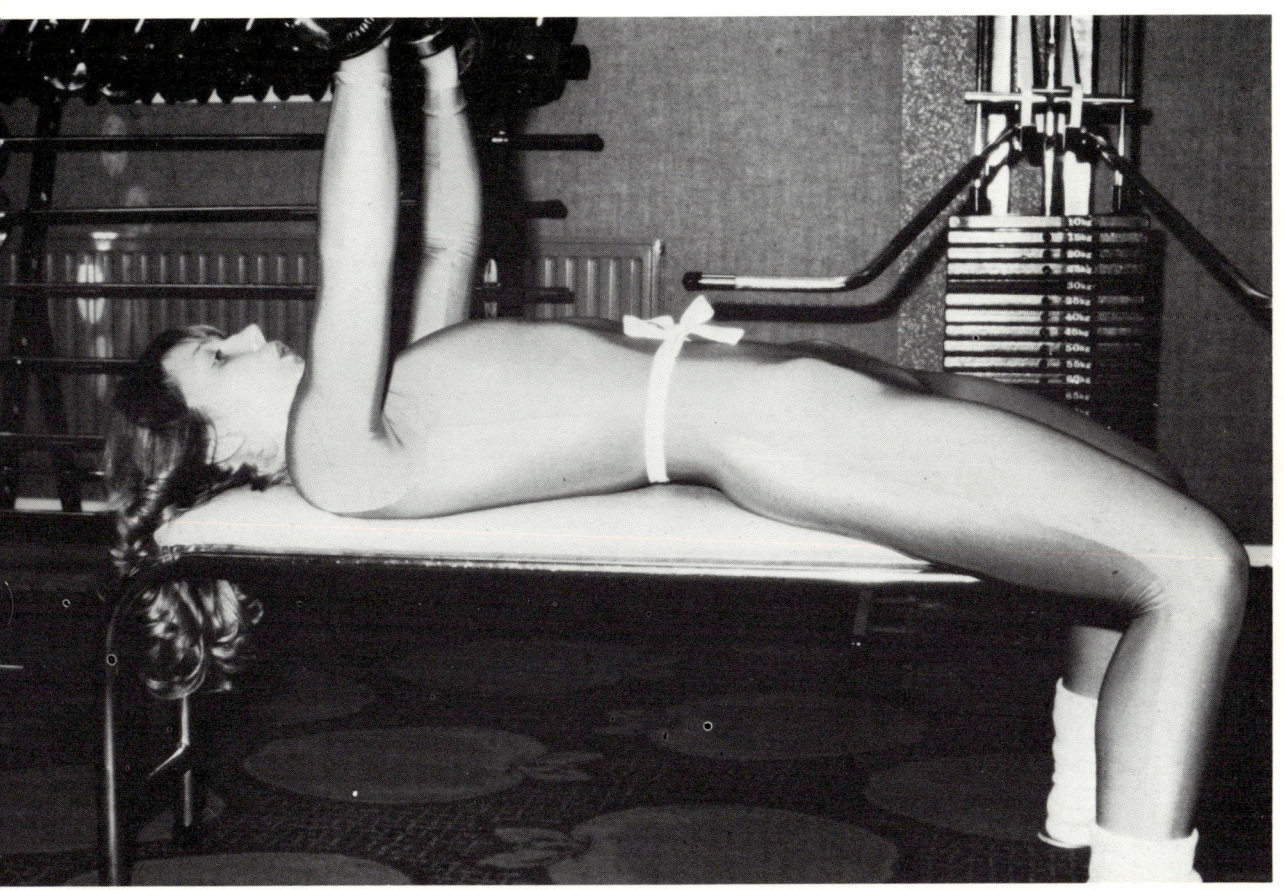

competitors if they wish to realise their full potential. There are many variations to the bench press — and I have used them all — but by now you should be realising that I have a very detailed approach to each body part. In the chest I see a need for a deep wide rib cage, and so I include exercises for encouraging this. I attack the pectorals from all angles, including work to build mass and definition, and I never neglect to develop the *top* part of the pectorals as well as exercising the more responsive lower area.

## CHEST WORKOUT
○ Flying exercise (preferably after leg work when there is a natural increase in respiration): 3 sets of 15 reps.
○ Bench press: 3 sets of 20 reps.
○ Incline bench press: 3 sets of 20 reps.
○ Dumb-bell declines: 3 sets of 15 reps.
○ Pec deck: 3 sets of 20 reps.

These, then, are some sample body-part workouts for experienced bodybuilders on their way to the top. Remember each is *part* of a full schedule, not a night's training on its own. This sort of regime is tough. It will work, but only provided that you do. Your results will be proportional to your efforts.

## 6 Nutrition for bodybuilders

Bodybuilders have been pioneers of the application of nutrition in heavy physical activity, and some amazing results have been achieved. A comparison of magazine photographs taken over the decades will show that muscular definition and sharpness of contours have improved tremendously in recent years and, whereas in the past one could just trace the outlines of the muscles, nowadays the very striations of the muscle fibres can be seen almost from their origins to their insertions.

I have my own very personal ideas on diet, and they will surprise a great many people — for example, during the last twelve months I have eaten hardly any red meat. But more about that and other sources of protein later.

A comprehensive and rational approach to diet is absolutely essential to every bodybuilder in the quest for an outstanding physique as it is a 'banker'. Good diet safeguards health and ensures the good work capacity which is so necessary for productive workouts.

The energy expenditures of bodybuilders are beyond the comprehension of the average person, so doctors may tend to scoff at my recommendations — for example, the vast amounts of vitamins I advise. I would simply say to the sceptical that they should try to follow me through a workout, even with very much scaled-down weights, before they criticise something about which they know very little.

### Protein requirements
Bodybuilding results in a great expenditure of protein, and after training large quantities of the products of protein dissociation (nitrogen, etc.) are excreted in the urine. In order to replenish stocks and lay down good functional muscle there must be a correspondingly large intake of protein.

Bodybuilders up to 12½ stones (80kg) will require about ½₃oz (1¼g) of protein to every 1 lb (0.45kg) bodyweight. Those who are over this weight, while obviously requiring more, do not have to have quite as much per pound bodyweight.

The daily diet of a person doing heavy training with weights should contain at least 10½ – 14oz (300 – 400g) of lean-meat or equivalent items. At this stage I must come back to my remark about red meat. Although things such as steaks are popular and beneficial, and liver has exceptional nutritional value, I still much prefer to get my protein from such things as chicken, turkey, fish and prawns, although strangely enough I am not too taken with the bodybuilders' favourite — tuna fish. White tuna is all right, but I find it more expensive and quite hard to obtain in Britain.

Carbohydrate is also necessary, although many shy away from this. Carbohydrates are the chief energy-producing nutrients and are necessary for body growth and function. The best sources are of vegetable origin: grains, flour, fruits (which I love) and potatoes (which I never touch).

### Supplements
It is not advantageous to the bodybuilder to consume huge quantities of food in order to obtain all the nutrition necessary for prolonged and intensive workouts, and I am quite adamant that vast quantities of supplements are not just desirable but essential. I take a full range of vitamins — not just multivits, which I consume in quantity, but also vitamins C, $B_1$, $B_3$, $B_6$, $B_{12}$ and $B_{15}$ (even although it's a bit controversial at the moment), and I dig into desiccated liver tablets, brewers' yeast and kelp. I take these for three months at a time, followed by a three-month break, so for a total of six months a year my normal food intake is heavily supplemented. Of the more than forty vitamins which have now been identified (although the effect of some on the body is still not known), the ones of particular interest are the ones I have mentioned.

The B-group vitamins are water-soluble.

Some 2 – 3mg of vitamin $B_1$ (thiamine) is used daily by the average person. The bodybuilder requires around 10mg, although only 1.5 – 2mg is to be found in the average diet. This vitamin promotes growth, aids digestion and is required for metabolism.

$B_3$ (niacin) eliminates mental depression and is an essential part of the enzyme system. 100mg per day is required in training.

There is about 1.5 – 2mg of $B_6$ (pyridoxine) in the daily intake; with large intakes of protein this should rise to 3 – 4mg. $B_6$ assists you to assimilate food and aids fat and protein metabolism.

The normal diet has not nearly enough $B_{12}$. Russian weightlifters have had injections of 100 – 200mg per day, as this has led to significantly increased work

# NUTRITION FOR BODYBUILDERS

ability and muscle strength.
I prefer to take mine in pill form and use daily. $B_{12}$ (cobacom, or cyanocobalamin) is known as the red vitamin and increases physical vigour and promotes growth; a deficiency leads to tiredness.

Of vitamin C (ascorbic acid) the body requires 50–75mg daily. However, if this is increased to 200–300mg, work capacity is enormously increased.

A word or two about desiccated liver would not be out of place. Often described as a wonder-food, it has great anti-fatigue properties. There have been some very impressive research results substantiating the value of this form of nutrition: one American authority claimed a 300 per cent increase in endurance as a result of desiccated liver tablets. I would not quote any precise figure, but I do know that they help me greatly through a vigorous workout, and I much prefer to consume a few tablets than have to chew my way through huge quantities of food to get just the same amount of goodness. The liver is concentrated by being dried in a vacuum at low temperature: all the goodness is preserved and concentrated into a quarter of its usual size, and as a result this form is far superior to cooked liver. One of the benefits is increased endurance to help you through your workouts; it also helps your body to neutralize certain unwanted chemical effects of certain foods and medicines.

Kelp is a treasure from the sea, containing more iodine and trace elements than any vegetable grown on dry land. Kelp has been very effective in treating bursitis, arthritis, ligament strains, skin complaints, etc. Kelp burns body fat and is a thyroid food (the thyroid gland functions to maintain metabolism balance). I find this natural nutrient from the ocean a great addition to my diet. Unfortunately, the body cannot retain huge quantities, so any surplus cannot be stored for future use.

## A personal diet

You will be thinking that with all these supplements I must rattle when I squat but, believe me, I need them, and *so do you if you train as hard as you should to reach maximum potential.*

In general terms, I am careful about what I eat at meal-times. I take little in the way of starchy foods, rice maybe twice a week, cakes very seldom. If I take ice cream I limit it to a couple of spoonfuls, and if I have one bar of chocolate in six months that's something of an event.

I take green vegetables regularly but find that salads don't seem to fill me. I get the impression they speed my digestion, and I would rather take an extra helping of chicken than have chicken and salad!

Eggs feature quite prominently in my diet; and, while I do not drink beer, I take spirits occasionally, and in moderation, preferring bacardi or brandy.

However, I am not recommending these to you as bodybuilding aids! I am simply trying to give you an insight into my personal likes and dislikes.

Looking at my nutritional lifestyle I find that — leaving the house as I do at 6.30am — I do not feel like breakfast. However, at 11.30am I have a meal of, for example, turkey and a couple of pounds of grapes. Two hours later I like a whole chicken — the bigger the better — and some fruit such as grapefruit, oranges or apples. Fruit juice is all I will have to drink at this time. In the afternoon, if I feel peckish I will have more fruit, but otherwise I have nothing else until my main meal of the day, which I have after training is over.

I thoroughly enjoy seafood and feel it is beneficial. In particular I like prawns, and my favourite fish is salmon.

I have tried to be perfectly frank and honest about my own diet, even including parts which may be controversial, because I do not wish to be hypocritical and also, simply, because I think the details show that, although I am careful about my diet, I do not carry it to the stage of being a crank.

One last thing. When a competition is approaching and you are dieting very strictly, it has a severe psychological effect: you will perhaps become very edgy and irritable. Remember that you owe it to the people you live and work with not to let this get out of hand.

# 7 Drugs

There is nothing new about people using artificial substances in an attempt to improve their capabilities. It was done in ancient times to enhance performance in battle, and regrettably for well over 100 years drugs of one kind or another have been used in sport. More recently, the use of drugs has become one of the most discussed topics in weightlifting and bodybuilding as well as in athletics and a great many other forms of sport. Make no mistake about it: although the media often focuses attention on bodybuilding drugs, these substances are very widely used in other forms of physical activity. It is a subject fraught with problems and extremely difficult to resolve.

Unfortunately nowadays even beginners, picking up snippets of gym gossip, contemplate using such things as anabolic steroids. To these young people I would give very emphatic advice that they should not embark on any such programme.

Indeed, this applies to any bodybuilder, young or old. Any bodybuilders who are considering such 'assistance' must realise that there are several different reasons not to take drugs.

- There is the legal side of the business. The buying and selling of drugs, including steroids, is subject to the laws of the land. These are frequently broken in the peddling process.

- Where this is the case there is sometimes a black market, blatant commercialism and cheating.

- Apart from the legal side, there are sporting rules which must be considered. Bodybuilders ought never to break these rules.

- Apart from legalities and rules, there is the ethical problem of whether it is right or wrong to gain advantages or improvements in this manner.

- The health angle must not be overlooked. Although under medical supervision and with properly controlled doses there may not be significant detrimental effects immediately, the long-term effects of even modest doses must not be overlooked.

Let me make it quite clear that drugs such as anabolic steroids will not in themselves build competition-calibre muscle for bodybuilders; experiments in America have proved that conclusively. However, further studies by the same investigators, O'Shea and Winkler, using the same subjects, showed that with high-protein dietary supplements there was decided improvement in performance. In addition, very heavy exercise as outlined in this book is still essential. There are no shortcuts.

# CONTEST PREPARATION

## 8 Contest preparation — peaks and troughs

It would be great if we could progress steadily from one contest to another, improving according to the amount of work we have done. Unfortunately, life is not like that, and bodybuilding is no exception to the rule. Sometimes progress is good and at other times it is slow and even nonexistent. Sometimes by working too hard we encounter the phenomenon known as staleness, and we may even feel that we are moving backwards instead of forwards.

There are reasons for these things and, by knowing the facts, we can adapt and adjust so that when that all-important event arrives we have peaked to top form.

Although life is full of ups and downs, I try to keep in good form physically and never to let myself get out of shape, in the way that some of the other leading contestants do. Promoters seem to know this, and on many occasions I have been asked to stand in for someone who has let the promoter down at the last minute. This book outlines the methods I use to keep myself in competition condition; in this chapter I shall talk about the factors which must be considered in order to avoid the troughs and about how to add that little bit extra as the contest approaches so as to peak at the right time.

Bodybuilding is a science, and the diagram shows how I see the long-term scientific approach towards major titles.

First you must build a base of fitness. The vast majority of champions in our game are very fit people — they have to be in order to cope with the amount of work necessary to build up their muscles to prize-winning proportions. As I have said, I do over 1,200 repetitions daily, many with extremely heavy weights, and that requires not only strength but also muscular and cardiovascular endurance. If anybody doubts the fitness needed, I have a standing invitation as already noted: try to follow me through a workout, even with scaled-down weights. You must build up to this level of fitness, and your early workouts should have this very much in mind; you are laying a foundation which is absolutely essential if you are to build the structure you are after — a Mr Universe physique.

The way to lay the kind of foundation required is to gradually increase your number of repetitions with all the standard exercises, and not to worry too much about pure strength. A much respected old-timer, Siegmund Klein, used to say: 'Train for shape and strength will follow.' That fits in well with the concepts which I shall now describe.

Having first produced a good basis of fitness by building up the muscles' capacity to cope with repetitions, you must now build strength by using heavier weights. Muscles are built by the 'overload principle', which means simply that they become larger and stronger only when required to perform tasks that are over and above previous requirements.

You now have two elements: repetitions, which can be thought of as the *volume* of your workout; and the weights used, which can be termed *intensity*. Volume is produced by the number of exercises, the number

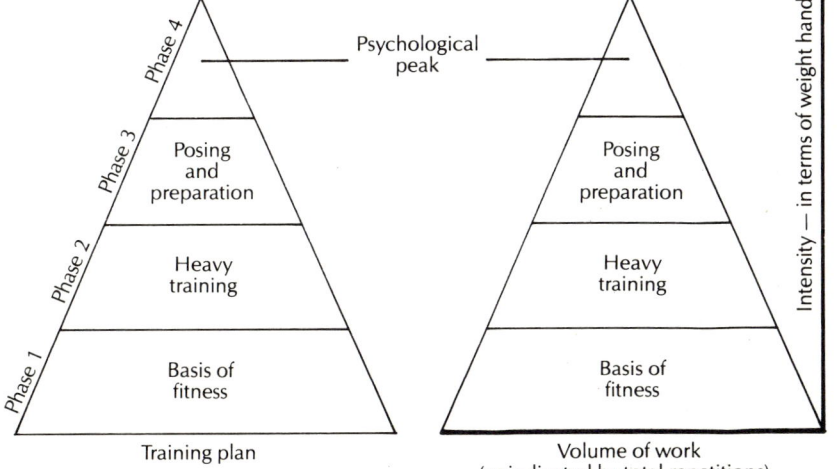

Diagrammatic representation of major elements in Bill Richardson's training philosophy and planning.

Training plan

Volume of work (as indicated by total repetitions)

of sets of each exercise, and then the number of repetitions in each set. You can progress first by adding repetitions and/or by adding sets, and then you can add weight and slightly reduce the number of reps., or, alternatively, you can do the same number of reps. and add another set. You can see that the science of bodybuilding is to achieve the correct balance of exercises, sets, reps. and weights to produce the result you want; there is a high degree of flexibility, which does not exist in other sporting spheres.

By keeping records you will be able to see exactly what suits you and what does not produce results.

Your pyramid towards a competition should gradually build up. As the contest approaches, I introduce another element of which most trainers are unaware. I bring in the progression of pace. This aim for speed is yet another calculated progression. The overall target is now to complete the full workout in a shorter time than before, and there are several different ways of doing this without cutting down on work — indeed, effort is significantly increased. You try to do each repetition faster, and this builds *power* — because power is the strength and speed you need to give velocity. By cutting the time of each rep. by even a fraction, the time for each set is significantly decreased. I then also try to cut down on the recovery time between sets. Finally, you can cut down on the negative-resistance work, the slow lowering of weights, so that you are pumping the weights faster throughout the routine. This is a very energy-consuming regime, which should not be sustained for lengthy periods of time, but it works wonders in bringing you nearer to the peak.

The idea of peaking on a single day is often overstated and overdone. I build myself to a physical plateau, using the techniques outlined, and on top of that plateau are added detailed personal preparation and a psychological peak at the exact time of my choosing. I am then contest-ready.

I realise that not everybody can duplicate my ability to remain in competition shape for long periods of time, and to those who cannot I would say that you should *plan* your peaks and troughs rather than leaving things to chance. Select two major targets: your main competition for your highest pinnacle, and a subsidiary target a short while earlier. After the first competition, ease off a little before coming back with renewed vigour for your onslaught on the major title — Mr Britain, Mr Universe, or whatever it may be.

## Pitfalls on the way to the peaks

Sometimes we just don't feel like training. Everybody is alike in this respect, but the various methods people use to treat the dilemma are radically different.

Personally I never allow myself to be influenced by such feelings. Instead I hurry and change, warming up quickly because I know that, as the blood begins to course strongly through my veins, I will feel better immediately, and that as the workout progresses I will forget the lethargic feeling. Those who succumb to the ailment will find that the thought of hard work becomes less and less attractive, until they reach the stage that, when they feel like exercise, they lie down until the feeling passes!

Some people wonder why we should have such ups and downs in daily life, and some very convincing theories have been advanced concerning biorhythms, the rhythmic fluctuations of the body. Experts in this field point out that in all life, in virtually every aspect of nature, there are cycles. The tide ebbs and flows every 12½ hours, the moon reappears every 25 hours, women experience the menstrual cycle over each 28 days, and so on. Research has shown that human beings display definite biorhythms, which determine our feelings and actions, in three cycles of varying lengths.

The 23-day *physical* cycle affects such factors as strength, energy and endurance. In the first 11½ days a person is likely to feel physically good, and physical work seems easier; the 2nd to the 9th days are considered best of all. The most critical times when a person is likely to be physically below par are on the first day of a

## CONTEST PREPARATION

new cycle and at the changeover after 11½ days.

The 28-day *emotional* cycle affects cheerfulness, optimism and, important to bodybuilders, coordination connected with the nervous system.

The 33-day *intellectual* cycle is less important to us except on the critical cross-over days.

There are certain times when these cycles coincide at high and low points to make us feel particularly good or particularly low. When you cross the physical base-line you feel less good than usual, but this will pass almost unnoticed. Trouble is said to be worse when you have a 'double critical' — that is, on the critical days when you are low in two of the three cycles (for example, you may be low both physically and emotionally as well). If, as happens about once a year, you have a triple critical, being low in all three cycles, then this is when you are most likely to skip training, be subject to human error, or have a violent argument with someone near and dear to you.

It is quite easy to calculate the ups and downs of biorhythms by tables, slide rules and calculators; alternatively, professionals can make complete charts of your criticals and advise you on training, decision making, etc.

There is a lot of food for thought in such theories, but there remains a considerable amount of work to be done before bodybuilders can utilise biorhythms as simple and effective tools of their trade. The fixed dates of competitions, the requirements for dedicated and progressive training regardless of personal feelings, and a multiplicity of external circumstances all seem to have more bearing on the subject than do biorhythmic cycles. I stick to my advice that you should train consistently and regularly, constantly striving for improvement, rather than allow yourself to be sidetracked or to ease off — no matter how plausible the excuse.

There remains one final pitfall: staleness. Staleness is not so evident in beginners as it is in mature bodybuilders. It is undoubtedly a mental as well as a physical phenomenon. It can sometimes be detected in its early stages by a loss of weight often linked with emotional upset. Other symptoms include lack of appetite and insomnia, which in themselves would account for a drop in weight. Strangely enough, staleness can be passed on by other people if you are not careful, and there have been cases of whole teams of players going stale, usually in a losing season! I know of one occasion on which twenty players in a team lost over 100 lb (45.36kg) in seven days.

There are a number of ways of overcoming staleness. One can simply adjust the routine for a few workouts, not necessarily to reduce the amount of work but to vary it by, for example, reducing intensity using slightly less weight and adding volume with extra reps. or sets. A change of exercise also works wonders, but avoid developing what is known as a grasshopper approach, jumping from schedule to schedule without first fully deriving some of the benefits of your carefully planned routine.

The Ultimate Physique

# POSING

## 9 Posing

There is still some controversy over whether bodybuilding is a sport, a science or an art. That discussion is likely to go on for a long time, but there must surely be general agreement that *posing is an art*. It is an art that every competitive bodybuilder must master if he or she has ambitions to win major awards. Schwarzenegger considers he lost to Frank Zane because of his lack of posing ability. To neglect posing would be madness, for in the final analysis this is where you show your hard-earned physique to its best advantage, and if you have flaws they can be minimised and concealed by good posing.

### The basics of good posing

I summarise the requirements for good posing in the following way:

○ Selection of poses to suit (a) the physique and (b) the occasion, whether it is in front of judges, an audience or the camera or as a guest appearance.
○ Presentation of selected poses (moving in, moving out and holding a pose).
○ Muscle control: full contractions of some muscles, complete relaxation of others.
○ Blending the poses. The juxtapositioning of poses.
○ Appropriate music (if posing for an audience).
○ Good lighting.

Having mastered a wide range of poses and put a good routine together, that's not the end of the story. You must practise regularly to perfect your posing, and lack of practice will result in rough edges which will be spotted by the experienced eye. Lack of practice, in fact, is the most common reason for poor posing. I find it extremely difficult to understand why this aspect of bodybuilding should ever be neglected. A good posing session can be hard work, but it is also a rewarding experience.

You should periodically update your routine, making changes to meet new situations, and altering your music too. There are fashions and progress in posing as in everything else, and you do not need to go back to the days of Sandow to see that things have changed. The routines today are entirely different from those of just ten years ago.

### Planning your poses

Start by mastering the standard compulsory poses. Double-biceps, side-triceps, lat-spreads, trap-overs and side-chest are all necessary if you intend to stand before the judges. You will be amazed at the variations possible in these poses, so make sure they show you as you would like to be seen.

Study the interpretations of world leaders, remembering that although the pose may suit Mr Universe it may not suit Mr East Ardsley.

When you are selecting and practising poses, the mirror is a good aid — although you must practise also without mirrors, as there are none on stage. The camera is another selection aid which is often forgotten. You should look at every available pose photograph of yourself so that you can study your own physique from all angles before deciding which poses to use.

In devising a routine you need not use every pose ever invented. Too many people with mediocre physiques bore audiences because of lengthy routines. Pick poses to show your best points

101

and conceal your weakest areas, and leave the audience impressed and wanting more; avoid overstaying your welcome.

In putting the poses into sequence, plan to move gradually from one to the next, remembering that the audience are also looking at you between poses. So move in and out of poses with style and panache using hands, fingers and facial expressions to convey a good impression. It is difficult to move well from a direct front to a direct back pose, and therefore it is best to intersperse such full views with side or three-quarter poses, or with those incorporating twists from the waist. A smooth transition is much better than a radical movement such as a full about-turn.

## Displaying the body parts
Looking at the various body parts, we will start by considering the arms. If you have fine biceps, then flex them in your various poses. Good arms are a great bonus in posing as the most classical and graceful poses call for free-ranging movements instead of tight, cramped flexes with your arms squeezed against your body. If you have arms which do not rank with those of your colleagues then you should avoid postures like those of Sergio Oliva, with hands above the head or arms outstretched. In this case you should concentrate on the side-triceps and other similar poses.

Muscle control is very important in posing, and nowhere is this seen to better advantage than in the abdominal area. To show the abdominals, completely empty the lungs and lean back a little, shortening the distance between the rib-box and the pelvis. Some bodybuilders use their hands on their waist to draw the skin tight over the ridges of the abdomen and enhance definition. Those without good abdominals usually settle for an abdominal retraction. This is another muscle-control movement in which, the air being expelled from the lungs, the chest is thrust forward to create a partial vacuum and the tummy is sucked in, making a spectacular difference between waist and chest size.

The legs can be shown in more ways than other body parts so it is especially important that you know how to place them to your personal advantage. The contrast between thigh relaxation and contraction can be dramatically presented; it will be remembered how Reg Park would wobble his relaxed thigh with his hand and then tense up to make it rock hard, as if it were chiselled in granite.

With all this talk about muscle control and body positioning it is all too easy to overlook what is a most important part of posing — the expression on the face and the positioning of the head. The novice often looks down and keeps his face turned away from the judges and audience during his posing routine, a sure sign of inexperience and lack of confidence. The experienced poseur will keep his face in the light instead of in the shadows, glancing down only to emphasise a certain body part, as for example in leg contraction. He will change his expression from time to time, looking pleasant and pleasing, and avoiding at all costs a worried, grim or vacant look. All of us base our assessments of people on their attitudes as shown in their faces, and physique judges and audiences are no exception.

## Music
You should carefully consider the choice of music for your poses, and if music and movement are not your strong points then get some advice. Indeed, even if you are confident of your own abilities in this line it is still a good idea to discuss the matter with others, as tastes vary so much.

My wife has had a considerable influence on this part of my presentations, and she has helped add a new dimension to my posing. My routines had been copied so much that, even when I did them in their original form, they seemed to be losing their appeal. I found it disconcerting to discover my favourite poses, their method of presentation and even my favourite music used more than once before I went on to do guest spots in shows, so I had to devise a completely new approach, and it was here that my wife was most helpful.

Between us we put together a very original routine with a combination of tunes, using music with varying moods and tempos. If anyone copies this, it will very obviously be a rip-off and will harm their reputation. Originality is well worthwhile, and the fame of many champions such as Corney, Coe and Makkawy has been largely based on unique posing routines.

Remember that the music for your poses puts the final polished professional touch to your physical presentation, and that to be successful you must have music to suit your physique, background and personality. Albert Beckles, Johnny Fuller and Bertil Fox find reggae appropriate because of their roots. The popular classics have long been utilised for posing routines, probably starting with Reg Park and 'The Glass Mountain', and more recently bodybuilders like myself immediately think of Serge Nubret when the theme from *Exodus* is played. It is my view that such grand music is suited only to grand physiques, and that the grandeur is completely out of place if there are not dignity and feeling in the posing.

'The Big Country' has been overused by some under-equipped competitors.

One (now retired) muscle controller used a fine piece of classical music to accompany his act. However, I found this ludicrous, because the controls often drew exclamations, titters and giggles which were quite out of keeping with the mood of the music. On the other hand, the tune 'Wheels', used by Tony Holland in a similar act, was just right.

One must avoid being too 'gimmicky', and the shadow boxing in one of Boyer Coe's routines to 'The Eye of the Tiger' drew a mixed reception. I personally did not think it suited him as well as some of his earlier efforts.

If you are a really good mover, then do not hesitate to include some dance rhythms. When moving from one pose to another, think and act like a dancer, with all your moves choreographed to synchronise perfectly with every note. A bouncy number and a bouncy routine are much enjoyed by the fans if well put over. The dancing connection is not limited to modern or disco numbers, and one of the all-time great poseurs, Ed Corney, took ballet lessons to improve his posing. He posed to the song 'My Way', made famous by Frank Sinatra.

In the time of Bill Haley, nobody dreamed of posing to rock'n'roll or any such pop music of the day. Now attitudes have changed and you get everything from the classical routine of Chris Dickerson to the most up-to-date up-tempo rhythms of the 'with it' bods.

In my posing routine of the moment I use six tunes to cover all the elements covered in this section. These tunes are: 'Shaft', 'Fame', 'Electric Avenue', 'See You Later, Alligator', 'The First Time Ever I Saw Your Face', and 'Red, Red Wine'. Don't copy these, though, or everybody in the game will recognise you for what you are — a rip-off merchant.

If music and movement are not your strong points then get some advice on the subject, but do remember that, if you do your own thing, expressing your own personality, you will rise above the run-of-the-mill copycats and stereotyped routines seen at every contest. You *can* develop posing sense and you *can* improve flow, rhythm and interpretation. Get involved with your audience and work hard for them, and in return they will stimulate you. I'll almost give blood if the fans give me great encouragement, as is so often the case.

**Poses**
*To take you step by step through a posing routine, explaining every detail, would not be a good thing. I would be failing in my duty to encourage you to be creative, and would deprive you of the satisfaction of devising your own personal posing routine. Instead, therefore, I make here some suggestions for poses and changes and show you how to move from one pose to the next. Treat these moves as individual small segments of a posing spot, and remember that, although these photographs are static, you must use music and movement in a*

# The Ultimate Physique

dynamic *way to make the best use of the short time you have on the platform. Share with me my poses and some of the random thoughts with which I accompany them.*

It can be very lonely on this posing plinth under the strong, all-revealing light. I'll have to work hard for their applause.

Let's show them some shape. Slowly *with the hands, away from the sides, tensing the lats as the music swells . . . S-p-r-e-a-d — wider.*

Yes, they like it! Now, hands on the hips to push in. Spread more — more. Now crunch those abs, put my hands to my thighs and work just a bit of the traps — keep some for later.

I feel my face relax and my smile widen . . .

POSING

*I transfer the weight to the left and shoot up a single biceps, turning my head to the flexed right arm. The emotion is beginning to flow, and I feel the warmth coming across the footlights from the auditorium as the clapping increases. It's a happy sound. All those hours of sweat and strain are paying off.*

*Smoothly now, into the double-biceps pose. Flex harder — harder. Make your body talk, man. The people out there hear it!*

*Change the mood. Glide the left arm upwards and relax the hand into a classic single biceps with semicontracted abs. Make a statement with the action: the body is beautiful.*

*Torso time. Squeeze down and shorten the trunk — work not just the abs but the obliques, intercostals and serratus, too. Raise the ridges, deepen the hollows. Slide down the hand. The audience is sure being good to me tonight.*

*Now the other hand and crunch those abs. Crunch again. I'm as happy as the people out there are . . .*

The Ultimate Physique

*Hit the single-biceps, and flex the left pec. Square up — solid, flat on the feet: a double-biceps with no frills. Peak those arms — peak!*

*The music and the mood are changing; serious again. Hands behind my neck and I swing my hips, sink and lean, keeping graceful and moving smoothly. The variations are essential.*

POSING

*Pivot slowly for a series of back poses. Some muscle, some with grace, all with class and style. Move the arms — make those snakes wriggle under the skin.*

Beef it on the strong bars and glide on the soft ones. Hit, 2, 3, 4; g-l-i-d-e, 2, 3, 4. And now back to face those lovely people.

They're yelling now as I momentarily lower my arms but keep the flex. Hold them! Give them more . . .

Hands behind my back and the pump is growing. The music is reaching a crescendo but I don't want to stop. Let it go on. Hit the 'crab'. Bring over those traps! Abs! Pecs! Everything! I swear those veins will burst.

But the sound is gushing, too. It's deafening me.

Thanks. Thanks. Thanks!

## Photographic physique studies

Most of the advice given here has been for competition or on-stage posing, so I will conclude with a few comments on the other aspect — photographic physique studies. Many of my earlier remarks relating to the selection of poses are equally true of a session in front of the camera. Be sure to pose to the best of your ability, because the lens is much more critical than the mirror. To make the most of photographic posing, be sure to get the cooperation of a photographer who knows how to depict the physique, especially with regard to lighting. Even with a good photographer, use commonsense and care.

Nude posing should be avoided on almost all occasions, no matter what the photographer may say. Such poses are seldom used in genuine physique magazines at the present time, and some enthusiasts have later regretted being photographed without posing briefs, which when properly cut can actually enhance the physique.

If a good physique photographer is not readily available, then a competent camera enthusiast with good equipment can be utilised for an outdoor session. Outdoor pictures have a much greater appeal than ineptly lit indoor studies. Use attractive, uncluttered backgrounds without too many distractions; sea and sand, or low-angled shots with plenty of sky, are popular and relatively simple. Wherever you are, make sure that the general area is tidy and not spoiled by having rubbish, clothing or other such items lying around.

Attention to detail can make all the difference between good pictures and mediocre ones, so train hard to build a good body, practising assiduously to master your presentation. Learn exactly where to stand under the lights; too far forward and you will be in shadow, too far back and you will flatten. Be meticulous in your personal preparation and then, by using the advice in this section, you should be able to show your physique to the greatest advantage whether you are posing for a live audience or for the all-seeing eye of the camera.

# 10 Positive thinking

CAN'T is a four-letter word bodybuilders should never use. There are a number of old sayings which give positive advice in different ways. 'Don't cut off your nose to spite your face.' 'If you want to get honey don't knock over the beehive.' 'Never cut off another person's legs to make yourself appear taller.' Unfortunately, a great many people go through life with a negative attitude which is reflected in their negative actions, instead of devoting their energies to self-improvement.

It does good to let off steam now and again and, as you will see in these pages, I believe in speaking my mind without fear or favour; but my overriding philosophy is one of a positive approach to living. Life is too short for trouble and strife, hassle and heartache; and there is a lot we can do to avoid getting into distressing situations. When I am working I just can't bear to waste time listening to a training companion gripe about a competition result or of how they have been ripped-off by some food-supplement dealer. I find it very much easier to share the joy of a successful competitor or to listen to and benefit from information about good equipment. In other words, I can soak up happiness, contentment, interest and enthusiasm. And when I assist people at the gym I like to instil them with self-confidence and self-respect: this can help them in bodybuilding almost as much as teaching them a new exercise or training principle

However, one cannot live in a vacuum and so, if unwanted emotions do encroach, then these should be used and channelled towards your particular training goals rather than be allowed to gnaw away and create frustration. It is quite amazing how anger, revenge, excitement, rage and even conceit can all be directed to assist and motivate a bodybuilder.

As a general principle, however, the negative feelings should be avoided. The greatest enemy of all is fear — fear of failure, fear of obscurity, even fear of being able to handle success. Fear of *any* form is undoubtedly your worst enemy, and the best way to overcome it is to study your fears as rationally as possible, face up to them, and see if they are really worth worrying about. If they are, then you must do something about these worries: work harder at training; enlist the aid of an understanding coach, instructor or training partner; get a shrewd adviser — anything to improve the situation. The mere fact that you are doing something about it will help a lot.

## The goal of improvement

One of the main rules in my bodybuilding regime is that I constantly strive for improvement. No matter how far ahead of the opposition I may be, I keep on trying to make my body better. I want to go before the judges in physically better shape than I was the time before, and the only way to do this is through a methodical progression and a deeply instilled desire for constant improvement.

Sometimes you may go to the gym feeling a little tired and not relishing the thought of a hard workout; we all feel like that occasionally. However, I never succumb to the desire to miss a workout, and when the blood begins to course through my veins I feel much better. As the pump progresses I feel elated; and I am glad that I overcame that initial lethargic feeling.

So much is in the mind. When you are feeling a little lazy, that is the time to get into your track suit as quickly as possible and get stuck into the weights without delay. Avoid pausing to discuss last night's TV shows or listening to the boys talk of last night's bird. When I am accosted with such diversions I try to be sympathetic and smile, saying something to the effect that it all sounds very interesting and I must hear all about it *after my workout*. Those last three words are very important, but they need not be said emphatically unless the distracters have hides like rhinos. Often a nod, grin and a 'let's finish this' are sufficient to communicate the message. The people around the gym soon get to know who are the gossips and who are really serious about their training and don't like having small talk, debate or erudite muscle-rapping between sets.

I don't wish to overemphasise the genial approach, but I do feel it is important not to lose your cool and snub someone: that doesn't do either of you any good. Although at one time it was a bit of an effort to hang loose when I was being bombarded with inane chatter, I can now walk away from it with a wisecrack and without giving offence.

In the same line, I can find time within my workouts to assist and

# POSITIVE THINKING

*Opposite: Absolute concentration during exercise*

advise others without in any way distracting from my own efforts. It doesn't take much energy to 'spot' for a kid doing squats or to lift on a bar for someone for a bench press between my own sets; nor does it hinder me to do what I see as casual coaching — 'Keep your back flat. Come on, just two more, one more. Well done.' Actually, I believe this helps me rather than holds me back because I feel good when I see that my encouragement is appreciated. Being honest, though, I have to say that I do not allow these interludes to interfere with my own workouts.

The rewards from this sort of positive attitude are sometimes more tangible than the warmth of feeling I get on these occasions. There has never been any shortage of assistants to help me, whether in loading weights, being spotters, or providing extra weight for donkey calf-raises. Yet I notice that some champions don't have this sort of support — and it's nothing to do with lack of deodorants!

## Just a little bit more

Another aspect of positive thinking is in concentration during an exercise. Competitive lifters have developed this to a high degree, and so have many top bodybuilders. In my own training I make use of my powers of concentration all the time in order to attain the targets I have set myself.

As I said earlier, to constantly improve one must constantly work harder. Muscles grow only through the 'overload principle'; i.e., they grow bigger and stronger to cope with progressively increasing loads.

If you stop increasing weights and repetitions, your muscles, having accommodated to the demands placed on them, will cease to improve. I must therefore keep striving for that extra rep., that extra set, or more weight, or more exercises. Of course, you can overdo any or all of these; but the beauty of weight-training is that you have the tools and the procedures to maintain the balance you require.

What you must also have is the concentration to force more out of your muscles than you did in your last workout. This may sound very hard — and that is exactly what it is. The muscles I carry did not grow without a lot of physical effort and mental concentration and a vast amount of positive thinking.

You are only what you believe yourself to be; it's all in the state of mind.

---

ALL IN THE STATE OF MIND

If you think you're beaten, you are.
If you think you dare not, you don't.
If you'd like to win, but think you can't,
It's almost a cinch you won't.
If you think you'll lose, you've lost,
For out in the world you'll find
Success begins with a fellow's will.
It's all in the state of mind.

Full many a race is lost
Ere ever a step is run,
And many a coward fails
Ere ever his work's begun.
Think big and your deeds will grow,
Think small and you'll fall behind.
Think that you can and you will.
It's all in the state of mind.

If you think you're outclassed, you are;
You've got to think high to rise.
You've got to be sure of yourself before
You can ever win a prize.
Life's battles don't always go
To the stronger or faster man.
But soon or late the man who wins
Is the fellow who thinks he can.

# 11 Psychology of competition

Arnold Schwarzenegger is rather fond of telling how he used to 'psyche out' his opponents in bodybuilding competitions. The whole psyching-out scene came through strongly in the bodybuilding documentary *Pumping Iron*, and I think it was this aspect which made the film distasteful to me — although I enjoyed the genuine bodybuilding contest and training sequences. Arnold boasts how he conned Sergio Oliva into leaving the stage during the pose-down in their epic contest and how he overwhelmed Lou Ferrigno, the 'Incredible Hulk'. The tactics were perhaps brutal by the normal standards of those days, but they were chickenfeed by comparison with some of the stunts I have seen pulled by American-based competitors.

They really play it rough. At a critical time these moronic characters will make very personal remarks simply to upset an opponent, and they do not stop at making comments about poor form, expanding waistline or shrinking muscles. On one occasion the fidelity of a bodybuilder's girlfriend was hotly disputed and in another a psycho freak said to one of his competitors: 'Hey man, I slept with your mother. Wow, is she great in bed.' It seems there is nothing sacred to these weirdos, for whom I have nothing but contempt. Of course, there must be contest psychology but I prefer a *positive* approach rather than the negative, destructive ploys of these creatures, who must crawl out from under stones to come and compete.

## Being psyched-out

First of all, I would like to assist the 'psyched-out' or hypersensitive bodybuilding competitor. These people are actually their own worst enemies. Whereas motivation is seldom a problem with them, the stress of training and competition is very real. They — we — revert to age-old behaviour patterns, where there is a tendency for either flight or fight. When put under strain before a big event we are apt to kid ourselves that we are uneasy, a little tense, perhaps ill at ease. We hardly ever admit to ourselves or anyone else that what we are feeling is honest-to-goodness fear — or, to put it another way, dread.

I like to avoid such extreme feelings, but if we consider them intelligently we can control and lessen these emotions and even put them to good use. Remember, you will never get a great performance without some such emotion leading to an increased flow of adrenalin.

The first thing to eliminate is any feeling of guilt about the fact that you are a little scared. There is nothing unmasculine about this — the toughest, most macho practitioners of the art of bodybuilding go through similar anxieties before major events. I am not a trained psychologist, but I will give you my advice for what it's worth. When you go to a contest, do not concern yourself too much with other competitors — how good they are, how they compare with you, and so on. Shut out such thoughts and instead concentrate on your own requirements and personal commitment to doing your very best in presenting yourself at every stage of the competition. Shut out undesirable factors around you and look only for necessary cues which will trigger off your performance: the marshals' or judges' instructions, your music, or the applause of the crowd. Develop poise and confidence in the knowledge that your personal pride will accept only the very best of efforts.

In passing, I should say that the over-anxious competitor is the one who is likely to peak too soon, and the more 'laid back' bodybuilder is the one more likely to peak too late. So find a balance.

## Psyching up

Having made certain that you are not going to be psyched out, you must next learn how to psyche up for major events.

Psychologists and physiologists are agreed that people can get a great deal of assistance from the proper functioning of the adrenal glands, which are situated near the kidneys. These glands are sometimes known as the 'fight or run' glands because at times of stress or in emergencies they prepare the body for action by increasing the heart and respiration rates and pushing up the level of energising blood sugar. This is why people become capable of jumping a gate to get out of the way of a bull, or a mother can generate enough energy to lift a heavy load pinning her child to the ground, or a highly motivated individual can single-handedly overcome tremendous obstacles of many different kinds.

When the amazing substance known as adrenalin is released into the bloodstream, a person becomes able to bring out hitherto-untapped resources, *but these must be controlled*. Sure, you want to be able to outpose your opponents in a pose-down and outmuscle them in a 'most muscular' trap-over type of pose, but you should not be so excited that you risk fouling up your carefully planned posing routine or destroying the mood or classic interpretations of your presentation to the judges and audience.

Mental control ranks alongside muscle control when the chips are down. To get the right degree of excitement and yet be calm enough to exercise judgement is no mean feat. However, like many other skills, this one can be cultivated. The ability to don emotional blinkers to shut out unwanted influences, and yet still to be able to use your supporters' or the crowd's encouragement to inspire you to greater efforts, is the hallmark of a champion.

When a competition day arrives, you should have everything planned in detail, and you should try to stick as closely as possible to arrangements, procedures and even tactics devised and thought out at a time when there was no pressure. Travel, eating, warming up — all should be gone over, so ensure that plenty of time is made available. However, you should also incorporate a degree of flexibility into your plans, so that if something doesn't go quite the way you expected it to there is an acceptable alternative.

If you intend to pump up, your routine should be planned and timed — and it goes without saying that you will have done everything possible to master your posing and will know everything possible about the judging procedure.

## How not to be psyched-out

The very fact that I have adopted a thorough approach like this in itself often puts my opposition at a disadvantage. If they ask me when I am going to begin pumping I will give them a smile and a wink or a nudge and tell them: "I brought my muscle with me!" I can sit and watch the strongest of my opponents sweating away, and they quite often get a little uncomfortable about being under such scrutiny; that does me no harm at all.

A friendly word here and a bit of praise there work wonders for me with those I know and trust, and if there are any of the bad-mouthed overseas brigade around they are welcome to try it on me, but they won't find an easy target . . . nor will they find me a Mr Nice Guy like Mike Katz. I am a lot more human, which in this context means I am less than perfect. Top-liners in the rough and tumble of international contest need nerves of steel, and I have toughened up to the required degree over the years.

If someone is trying to psych me out I don't mind taking them on, but I do it on my terms and only if I want to. Sometimes I will whip my shirt off and hit a couple of poses alongside them for comparison: I *know* that they won't outpose me. Maximum-effort posing can be tiring, but I have proved to myself that I have the endurance to cope with any demands of this kind — once I had to pose for just over an hour on stage to a variety of different records. On stage, or in front of the judges, there is frequently this competition to outpose each other, and there are so many ways of doing it.

If the judges call for a comparison pose of one body part you can easily, while adopting the pose requested, slip in transitional poses of some other muscle groups, thereby greatly adding to the overall effect. You can go through positions which show you to advantage during movement and, of course, when it comes to free posing you can hit more poses, outshine the others with your favourite poses, and play to the gallery in a variety of ways, milking their applause for you and letting everybody know that you are doing so.

# PSYCHOLOGY OF COMPETITION

*Confidence: I know they won't outpose me*

## 12  A final word

My task is almost over and it has been a labour of love. For a long time I have wanted to put something back into this activity which has meant so much to me: this book has given me that opportunity.

Writing for you has made me focus my mind on training in order to remember things I had almost forgotten or had started to take for granted, so I suggest that you do not read this book just once and leave it on the shelf. Pick it up again from time to time to refresh your memory, and reread what is most relevant to you at that particular stage in the training of your body.

I sincerely hope my advice will help you achieve your objectives, and I am certain that if you follow the instructions given you will make those dreams of a fine body come true. It is a quest which will not be easy, but do not give up when the going gets tough — dedication and determination will get you there in the end. The only failures in bodybuilding are the ones who drop out.

It would be churlish of me to overlook the great encouragement I have had over the years from my friends in bodybuilding, and I would particularly like to thank Oscar Heidenstam, NABBA secretary, who since my earliest days in the activity has been a guide, a mentor and a friend. His faith in my ability and his constructive comments have long been an inspiration. Without this sort of encouragement I am sure that I would not have pushed so hard in my training.

I cherish the friendship of officials such as Scotland's David Mitchell, who is another tireless worker for bodybuilding; and I am deeply grateful for the camaraderie which exists in bodybuilding and which is typified by competitors such as Roy Duval, Bill Hemsworth, Ian Lawrence, Eddie McDonough, Walter O'Malley and Terry Phillips, to name but a few.

Clearly I can never meet everyone who has read this book and followed my methods, but to those of you whom I may meet in competitions I say: please do give me news of your progress. Nobody will be more pleased than me to hear of the results you have achieved or the titles you have won.

May your training problems be as small as your muscles are large.

The Ultimate Physique

# Glossary of basic terms

**abs** see physique areas.

**cheating technique** In 'cheating style', other parts of the body in addition to the main working muscles are called into play in order to allow the handling of heavier weights, particularly in the inner range of muscle work, when the muscle is working at its shortest (and, often, strongest). A heave from the back or legs is frequently used to add momentum to the bar, so taking it through the middle range, which otherwise could often create a sticking-point in an exercise.

**clean** see lifting positions and movements.

**endurance** see physical qualities.

**flexibility** see physical qualities.

**flushing** The theory of this practice is that, by doing numerous sets, groups and exercises all for the same muscle group, the area in question becomes flushed with blood. A danger is that, if this technique is overdone, the muscle quality — in terms of both strength and ability — may be very suspect. Muscle built in this way often does not retain its size as well as better-quality muscle which has been built using more traditional methods.

**get set** see lifting positions and movements.

**glutes** see physique areas.

**grip** see lifting positions and movements.

**hang position** see lifting positions and movements.

**instinctive training** In this type of training the bodybuilder does the exercises he feels like doing at the time. Random training systems of this sort represent bodybuilding anarchy, since they lead to overconcentration on the trainee's favourite exercises rather than on the exercises he requires in order to develop his worst body-parts.

**isolated work** In this type of training there is a movement which involves only a single joint and a single muscle group. An example is the triceps stretch.

**lats** see physique areas.

**lifting positions and movements**
○ *clean*: This is the movement where the weight is pulled from the floor to the chest and shoulders in one uninterrupted motion. In the old ('continental') style, the bars were lifted first to the thighs, then to the belt, and finally to the shoulders; the French then introduced the clean lift, straight to the shoulders.
○ *get set*: The starting position for lifting the bar off the floor. Normally the spine is kept *flat* (which means not rounded: the term does *not* mean horizontal or vertical). In addition, the legs are bent so that, in this mechanically weak position, legs and back share the work.
○ *grip*: There are two main gripping positions. In the *over-grasp* the knuckles face forward. In the *under-grasp* the palms are forward. A variation is the *alternate grasp*, usually used only in dead lifts, in which one hand is in the over-grasp and the other in the under-grasp position.
○ *hang position*: Here the body is upright and the legs and back straight. The arms are straight and hanging by the sides, with the hands holding the bar. This is the starting position for the curl, the finishing position for dead lifts, and so on.

**military (strict) technique** Here the exercises are performed by the main working muscles alone. The adjective 'military' refers to the erect, upright position maintained in pressing, curling, and other standing exercises. In most strict-style exercises the starting position is maintained throughout the movement.

**pecs** see physique areas.

**physical qualities**
○ *cardiovascular endurance*: Fast recoveries between lifts or exercises require efficient heart, lung and arterial action. This condition is known as cardiovascular endurance and is a general condition, in contrast to muscular

# GLOSSARY OF BASIC TERMS

endurance (see below), which can be much more local.

○ *flexibility*: This term refers to the range of movement or joint mobility. The regular performance of exercises which work the muscles and joints from full extension to full contraction helps maintain flexibility.

○ *muscular endurance*: The ability to perform continuous muscular effort without undue fatigue is a characteristic of well trained, experienced bodybuilders. This quality is known as muscular endurance.

○ *power*: This is a combination of strength and speed. Fast explosive actions — as in the snatch — typify the use of power.

○ *strength*: In weight-lifting and physical-culture terms, strength is the ability to exert force in a single repetition. This quality is typified in squats and maximum dead lifts.

**physique areas** Bodybuilders often abbreviate the names of muscles or parts of the body; for example, the deltoids — muscles which cap the shoulders — are referred to as *delts*. While I urge you to learn the correct names, here are some of the commonest abbreviated forms:
○ *abs*: Abdominal muscles.
○ *glutes*: The gluteals, muscles of the hips: the gluteus maximus, gluteus minimus and gluteus medius.
○ *lats*: The latissimus dorsi, the

big showy muscle on the front of the chest.
○ *quads*: The quadriceps, the four-part muscle on the front of the thigh above the knees.
○ *traps*: The trapezius which, although a muscle of the back, is shown from the front in 'trap over' (most muscular) poses.

**power** *see* physical qualities.

**pre-exhaustion system** Introduced by the Canadian/British author Bob Kennedy about 1967-8, this principle recognises that many exercises involve more than one muscle. To gain maximum benefit, therefore, it is sometimes necessary to tire one of the muscles by ISOLATED WORK before going on to a heavier movement. For example, in a bench press the triceps usually give out before the pectorals. To overcome this, the pectorals are given isolated work (such as the flying exercise or lateral-raise lying) before the trainee goes on to bench presses. The chest muscles are thus 'pre-exhausted' and, if the amount of work involved in the first movement has been correctly estimated, will give out at about the same time as the triceps.

**quads** *see* physique areas.

muscle of the back which gives it the coveted 'V' taper.
○ *pecs*: The pectorals. The pectoralis major is the

**repetitions (reps)** This term refers to the number of times an exercise is done consecutively. The number of reps performed depends on the aims of the individual. Competitive Olympic and power lifters who require strength do low numbers of reps (1–5 times), while people seeking endurance do high numbers of reps (30–50). The numbers of reps done by bodybuilders vary between these extremes.

**sets** Although beginners may do only one set of repetitions, experienced weight-trainers do exercises in sets or groups of reps with a short pause for rest in between each set. This system makes for quality as well as quantity of muscle. It is possible to use heavier weights if you are doing, say, 4 sets of 15 reps than it would be if you were doing 60 reps without a pause.

**strength** *see* physical qualities.

**strict technique** *see* military technique.

**traps** *see* physique areas.

**unstructured routines** These routines are much like INSTINCTIVE TRAINING, except that here there is an overall plan, with certain body-parts being worked on specific days — for example, chest and legs on Mondays, biceps and back on Tuesdays, and so on.

# The Ultimate Physique

# Index

**A**
abdominal muscles (abs) 33, 58–64, 127
adductor muscles 33
alternate-arm dumb-bell press 45
alternate forward raises 47
alternate leg-raises 64
Amateur Athletic Union 25
apparel 29, 35
arm muscles 36–43

**B**
back muscles 64–73, 84
barbell curl 36–37
barbell press 45
barbells 48, 52–53, 65, 66–67
bench curls 39–40
bench presses 52–54
bent-knee raise see leg-raises
bent-knees sit-ups 59
biceps muscles 32–33, 36, 40, 84
biorhythms 98–99
bodybuilding exercises 34–81
bodybuilding in the future 26
bodybuilding in the past 14
bodybuilding today 14–16, 25–26
brachialis anticus muscle 36
breathing 29, 31
British Championships 7

**C**
cables 50–51
calf machine 80–81
calf muscles 79–81, 83–84
cheating curls 40
cheating technique 126
chest muscles 52–57, 84–85
clean lift 126
clothing see apparel
contest preparation 97–99
coraco brachialis muscle 36
cross-overs 64
crunches see squeezes
curve of effort 34–35

**D**
dead lifts 73–74
decline bench work 57
deep-knee bend see squats
deltoid muscles (delts) 32, 33, 44
depletives see tapering off
Deva, Andy 7
diet see nutrition
displaying the body parts 102
donkey heel-raise 79
drugs 88
dumb-bell bench press 54
dumb-bell curls 38–39
dumb-bell flying exercise 55
dumb-bell incline/decline press 56–57
dumb-bell presses 44–45
dumb-bells 43, 66

**E**
easy bar see EZ curl bar
effort see curve of effort
endurance 126–127
erector muscles 32, 73
European Championships 8
exercises see bodybuilding exercises
extensor muscles 40–43
EZ bar curl 37
EZ curl bar 40–41

**F**
Fédération Internationale Haltérophile et Culturiste 25
fitness see contest preparation
Fitton, Tony 7
flexibility 127
flexor muscles 32–33, 37–40
flushing 126

**G**
gastrocnemius muscle 32–33, 79
get set 126
gluteal muscles (glutes) 32, 127
good morning 73
grip 126

**H**
hack squats 77
hang position 126
heavy work 34
heel-raises 79–81
Heidenstam, Oscar 10, 125
hygiene 29, 35
hyperextensions 71

**I**
Inch, Tom 11, 16
incline bench work 56
instinctive training 126
International Federation of Bodybuilders 25
isometric work 34

**K**
kick-backs 42–43

**L**
lat pulley pull-downs 67
lat stretch pull-downs 70
lateral raise with cables 51
lateral raise with dumb-bells 46–47
latissimus dorsi muscles (lats) 32, 64–67, 127
Lawrence, Ian 9–10, 125
leg curls 76
leg extension 75
leg muscles 74–81, 84
leg presses 78
leg-raises 60, 64
lifting positions and movements 126
limbering up 34
lower back muscles 64

**M**
military press 48–49
military technique 35, 126
Mitchell, David 10, 125
muscle work 33–34
muscles 32–33, 36, 44, 52, 58, 64, 74, 79, 127
music (for posing) 102–103

**N**
National Amateur Bodybuilders Association (NABBA) 10, 25, 125
nutrition 86–87

**O**
organisations 25–26
other activities 31–32

**P**
Park, Reg 7, 11, 25, 103
peaks and troughs see contest preparation
pec deck 56–57
pectoral muscles (pecs) 33, 52, 56, 127
physique areas 127
physique studies 116
planning your poses 101–102
peroneal muscles 32
posing 97, 101–116
positive thinking 117–119
power 127
pre-exhaustion system 127
preacher curl 39–40
press behind neck 48–49
progression 31
protein requirements 86
psychology of competition 97, 117–122
pull-downs 67, 70–71
pulley rowing 68–69
push-down on pulley 40–41

**Q**
quadriceps muscles (quads) 32–33, 74, 127

**R**
relaxation 35
repetitions (reps) 29, 127
rest pauses 29
rhomboideus muscle 32
Richardson, Bill: a profile 7–13
rowing 65–67

**S**
sartorius muscle 33, 74
Schwarzenegger, Arnold 101, 121
Scott bench curl see preacher curl
seated dumb-bell press 45
seated heel-raise 81
seated twists 61
separation 14
serratus muscles 32–33, 52
sets 29, 127
short-range barbell press 45
shoulder muscles 44–56
side-bends 62–63
side raise see lateral raise
single-arm dumb-bell press 44
single-arm pull-downs 67
single-arm rowing 66
single-arm triceps stretch 43
single-end rowing 66–67
sit-ups 58–59
size of muscles 14
small muscle group exercise 34
soleus muscle 32–33, 79
specialisation 31
squats 74–75
squeezes 62
standing dumb-bell curl 38–39
static muscle work 34
straight-leg sit-ups 58–59
strength 127
stretching exercises 34
strict technique see military technique
supplements (nutrition) 86–87
symmetrical physique 14

**T**
tapering off 34
thigh muscles 74–78
tibialis anticus muscle 32–33, 79
training principles 29–35
trapezius muscles (traps) 32, 73, 127
triceps dips on chairs 42–43
triceps muscles 32, 36
triceps stretch 40–41, 43, 126
twists 61
two-arm dumb-bell press 45

**U**
unstructured routines 127
upper back muscles 64–66
upright rowing 47, 48

**V**
ventilation 29
vitamins see supplements

**W**
workout routines 82–85
World Bodybuilding Guild 25

**Z**
Zane, Frank 101

128